You don't know where I came from…

*One woman's story about overcoming struggle
and abuse: guided by faith to achieve success*

Barbara J. Condo

Published by Barbara Condo, Founder and Executive Director of One Way Farm
http://www.onewayfarm.org/

First paperback edition. Barbara Condo, 2010

Grateful acknowledgement is made to the following:
Cover design by Brenda Snowden
Edited by Kimberly Mitchell dba White Orchid Publishing
Stock photography courtesy of Dreamstime.com

For information regarding bulk purchases or any other needs, please contact Barbara Condo or the One Way Farm Children's Home at http://www.onewayfarm.org/

Printed in the United States of America.

Library of Congress Control Number: 2011913934

ISBN 978-0-615-5-2342-2

DEDICATION

I dedicate this book to Mike Toothman.

*Mike is an individual of great faith
who walked this walk with me,
spiritually and financially, to secure a home
for the lost and the abused and abandoned.*

INTRODUCTION

In this world, many children suffer abuse and humiliation. There are those who survive these unjust disadvantages and some who do not. One, such as the child in this book, looked to a higher power to achieve happiness and success in her life.

Barbara became a woman of faith; later realizing that all of her trials and humiliation would then become her formal education to work with children who tolerated the familiar scars that she had endured.

The walk of faith through this book shows that an ordinary person must rely on faith to change the world she lives in.

CONTENTS

Part One – From a Seed to a Bloom

Part Two – One Way Farm

You don't know where I came from…

Part One
From a Seed to a Bloom

Chapter 1
Through the Eyes of a Child

I turned the knob, but the door wouldn't budge. Maybe I should knock. Maybe she was inside, sleeping it off. No luck. Savagely, I kicked the door. Not being able to get inside meant that I had to climb in through the kitchen window over the stairwell. As my knees gripped the rough concrete ledge, I inched along to the corner of the window. Just as I reached for the window, I slipped. The rough dark bricks flashed past my eyes as I tumbled and hit my back on the bottom of the stairs. Just then, a window right above me opened.

"You dirty little brat! Tell your mother not to go away and lock you out." yelled a neighbor. I gasped for breath; fighting the pain and fear from the hasty topple to the ground. After what seemed like a long time, I crawled up the steps. Since there was no way inside, once again, I would have to scrounge for bottles in trash cans to get money for food, or maybe I would run through the alley to where the man who gives you a nickel if you let him kiss you lives. I was only an eight-year-old little girl at the time, and all I had ever known was loneliness, cold, hunger, abuse, humiliation, and deprivation.

My parents got divorced when I was four so this lifestyle wasn't new to me. Mother was an alcoholic; disappearing for days at a time and locking me and my brother out. She had a job in a defense plant during WWII. When she remembered to buy food, we ate. When she forgot, we didn't. Of course, when we did get to eat, we had to wipe the roaches off the plates first.

I remember being so cold from having no breakfast or dinner I would shake with a chill that was unbelievable. I often forgot about being cold, knowing that when I got to school, I would be in a place where it's warm. I recall many times when I would ask other kids if I could go home with them for lunch. "Hey, how about me going home with you for lunch? My mom won't care, she's working." The nice children were so afraid of me that they would never reject my request. I was uncomfortable in their homes, but getting a good meal was a necessity to survive for me.

Their parents would often say in low voices, "Why did you bring *her* home? I don't want you hanging around kids like that." They would look at me as if I had lice; which many times I did.

Yes, I do remember the pencil going through my hair; then the calling of names of those who had to go to the office. The kids laughing and yelling, "Get away, you've got bugs! Get away, get away!" I remember the *purple stuff* being applied; like putting salt in an open wound and the strong smell of sulfur in the air. Once, my mother had to shave my head to get rid of the lice! The mocking from the other children was a nightmare and there never seemed to be any shelter from such hate and humiliation. I was crying on the outside and the inside, "I want to be loved! Someone please love me!"

There were no guidelines on how life was supposed to go. No one was telling me what to do, where to go, or when. As a result, I became prey for all types of negative situations. Once, at the age of eight, a few of the neighborhood boys asked me to come up to the top of a garage. "Come on in, we ain't gonna hurt you." As I climbed up the steps, one of them grabbed me. To my surprise and shock, three of the boys were exposed from their waist down. They began grabbing and yelling, "Come on in! We're gonna show you what it's all about." I started to scream and cry so hysterically that they pushed me out of the top of the garage. I remember falling and falling. It seemed to take forever for me to hit the ground…almost as if it was happening in slow motion. Again, I was hurt, emotionally and physically, with no one to go crying home to. My only choice was to simply pick up my thin, shaken body and walk toward the dark grey apartment building where I lived. The musty smell, the yelling and cursing neighbors, fighting and loss were all part of my home environment. Hungry and crying for help, I climbed underneath a porch that smelled of urine from the nightly drunks who made this their bathroom stop. Soon, I would face another day…one with the same problems, the same hate, the same hunger, and no love.

In my world, sex was something everyone used for their own gain. There were people who talked about sleeping with their neighbors, others who were victims, and all of it was just something I didn't understand.

This place I called home had many frightening aspects. All around me there was filth of one kind or another. There were trash cans with rats as big as cats; squealing as you passed by. The hallways of our building were black as night; giving men even more opportunity to grab you with the intention of getting you to kiss them. Stealing was common place...even by me; for whatever I needed or wanted.

Finally, three years later, the court awarded custody of me and my brother to my father. Our lives improved somewhat, but as we soon learned my father's wife was also an alcoholic and very jealous of us. On Sunday mornings my dad would drop me off at church. Unfortunately, on one particular Sunday I came home to a raging fight. My stepmother started yelling at me, "You little flirt! You are just like your mother. You're a no-good tramp!"

From that moment on I was no longer allowed to kiss my father. Her reasoning for this jealousy was because I was wearing lipstick. She said it was wrong for a twelve-year-old girl to kiss her father hard enough to leave a lipstick print. My father yelled, "She is just a kid... and she's my daughter!"

I ran out of the house to a field which, unbeknown to me at the time, would become my prayer ground. Every time something went wrong, this is where I went, to cry, and ask God, "Why? Why is life like this?" As much as I appreciated my father trying to stick up for me, this moment was just the beginning of many painful memories to come. If only I had known that these experiences were just part of my education; a part that the Lord knew I could endure.

I distinctly remember the grass in this field. It was high like wheat, the color was golden, and the sun made it warm and soothing. I would lie down in the grass and make a nest for myself. With the warm sun on me, I would pretend that I was talking to someone who loved me...and often that was God. I felt important and loved there. The outside world could not enter this part of my life and I never wanted to leave. But, then again, I had to face life and had no real preparation for it.

At the age of thirteen, I wanted to go out on a Saturday night. My stepmother said I couldn't go out until I did all of the laundry and cleaned the house. When I finished she said I must cut the grass, too; knowing I couldn't get it done in time. The thermometer stood at 97.5° and sweat poured down my face. I remember the whirl of the blades, then dizziness, then the figures of my father and the family doctor standing over me. I just had my first convulsion. The doctor said, "She's okay. You know things like this sometimes happen to girls this age." The doctor left and my father and stepmother started to fight.

"I won't have anyone living with me that's gonna have fits!" she yelled. My father told me to get in the car and we would go for a ride. When we got back home, all of my clothes had been thrown into the road. I watched as cars passed, driving over the items that were once my only belongings.

"It's either her or me," bellowed my stepmother, and I knew she meant it.

Then it happened. My father came to me and said, "I'm sorry, but you will have to leave." He was the only person on earth I thought really cared about me and now he, too, had left me to my own defenses…and I was only fourteen at the time.

Next, I went to live with an aunt. In order for me to live there, I had to work in homes as a domestic. This allowed me to earn some money so I didn't mind. It was a lonely life though and the hours between school and work were getting to me. As time went on, it became very hard for me to go to school. I was getting very weak.

Eventually, I couldn't take the work load anymore. My illness started with a high fever and dizziness and for a good period of time I felt just awful. I remember standing in the hall at school, telling someone that I felt like I was going to pass out so I went to the office. Then the questions started, "Are you pregnant?" "Are you having sex?" "Who are you having sex with?" One person after another asked me the same questions. The experience brought back so many memories of my stepmother telling me that I would surely be pregnant by the time I was fourteen. With all of the commotion, I passed out.

Eventually, my condition improved with time and I was able to return to school. I decided to leave my aunt's house and figure out a way to make it on my own. Luckily, I did find a place to stay; it was an old attic. The people living in the house gave me permission to stay in the attic. So I found a mattress on the street, carried it upstairs, and made their loft my home. Besides the attic being dirty and lonely, my only source of heat came from the door being left open to downstairs where the family lived.

I found work at a seat cover factory and lived on my own. For me, this was a step in the right direction. I went wherever I wished, whenever I wished, and I forgot about God. In my desperation, I searched for real, permanent love from someone around me. I let go of God, but luckily He didn't let go of me. As the words in the song "Amazing Grace" (written by John Newton) goes, "How sweet the sound that saved a wretch like me...."

After a while, I knew something had to give. Between going to school and working at the factory, I was wearing down quickly. I knew I couldn't continue at the pace I was going. I went to school all day and worked from four o'clock to midnight; which included walking home ten blocks at the end of my shift. Since I couldn't keep doing both, once again, I had to move.

This time I had to move in with another aunt. She was a strong, impersonal German woman who was also cursed with alcoholism. With no other place to go, I agreed to do her housework in exchange for living there.

As time went on, my illness grew worse. My legs hurt unbearably. My joints started to swell and my throat was dry, parched, and burning. Next, I started getting chills and cold sweats, leaving me shaking in bed. It happened. I was broken physically and mentally. Soon after, I was completely bedridden, with no one to help, and no meals until sometimes late in the evening. The doctor had said it was rheumatic fever and that I should stay in bed. Now, how was I going to earn my keep?

One cold, snowy December night my aunt and mother sat in the kitchen drinking. They shared their thoughts about what to do with me. My aunt was angry because she had to keep me there, for I was no use to her. My mother believed that there was nothing wrong with me. They headed to my room and began yelling at me. I cried, tears running down into my ears. As they screamed at me, they began pulling at me to get up. With no strength left in my tiny body, I fell out of the doorway into a soft white drift of snow. It was cool and I wanted to lie there and die. All of my will to live was gone. Life was just too painful. If only I had known that to be in the world it is painful, but to be in Christ is to love. Finally, after several hours, my uncle came home and carried me back to bed. I could hear my aunt and uncle screaming back and forth over what transpired...until finally, I fell asleep.

Still on the path to find my one true love, I married at seventeen, was expecting a child at eighteen, and again at nineteen, and as one might expect, the relationship ended in divorce at twenty. With two babies in tow, I was alone in a world of sin. It was always men, sex, and money. I became so sick of all of it. I can still hear, "Come on, baby. We'll go to Miami this week. Get your mother to watch your kids. What is wrong with a little fun? Everybody is swinging!" Or "Hey, you got class. How about coming over to the motel? We've got some men coming in from out of town." In my mind, I am saying, "I hate this, leave me alone."

To escape this, and to obtain what I thought was secure love, I remarried. The second marriage lasted seven miserable years. Again, two babies are born and a second divorce is the conclusion.

What to do! Crying babies were endless, but I did love them so. Sometimes I feel I should kill them so they don't have to suffer like I did. "Someone just hold me!" I would say, as I shake throughout my body. I wanted to run, run, run! My nerves were broken. It was at this time that I entered the hospital for some help. The doctor said my condition was due to my childhood; that I was punishing myself for everything that happened to me. After several visits to the clinic, I told the doctor that I believed the only answer to a person's dilemmas was God. Just to say that gave me some freedom from my pain. It felt as if a load was lifted off of me. I finally knew where I needed to focus my energy.

At last, I felt a great desire to go to church. On the first Sunday I attended, I went forward for an altar call. I was saved and buried with Christ through water baptism.

> "Then life became *Life!*, for He came so that we might have life more abundantly. He whom the Son sets free is free indeed." (John 10:10)

In order to support me and my kids, I cared for fifteen to twenty children a day. I took care of the diapers, feeding, playtime, and runny noses; all of which ended with the daily mopping up of all the little ones. But praise the Lord; I came through it all with victory. For extra money, each week I would iron laundry for five different families and I also got quite good at setting hair for several of the women in the neighborhood. We were happy. As for me, this was the happiest I had ever been. Of course, the Lord had other plans for us; for children need a father and a woman needs a husband as head of the house. If only I had known how deep you can go with the Lord.

Instead of following the path to God, I started doing *uppers* to keep up with the pace...not believing this was wrong. I took one or two *Black Mollies* a day, which carried me through all the things I had to do. I went to church, worked hard every day, and tried my best to be a good mother. Still, there was something missing. I knew that it was the real commitment of my life to Christ. I might have His angels helping me, but oh, if I had the Holy Spirit, what a fuller life it would have been. For it is written,

> "For you shall receive power." (Genesis 14:3)

The Lord knew what He was doing and had plans for my life that became the miracles of grace.

Finally, I met the man of my dreams. We were very much in love, so we married on August 10, 1968. Since both of us had children from previous marriages, we had a full house of possessions from the start. We picked out the best furniture from each household and got rid of the rest. You never saw so many beds!

The Lord had this planned all along, but I didn't know it until then. Soon, we were going to church together as a family. No, we weren't perfect, but I did want this marriage to work and I knew that meant being ready for a lot of work.

I was very busy working on our house (trying to keep up with the Joneses). I always needed to have everything match; clothes, cars, furnishings. One time, I painted two of our rooms and there was blue and gold paint all over the place. Then, I started to paint another dresser apple green. I will never forget that color. It seemed to be everywhere I was! I finished the dresser drawers and had them lined up in the bedroom to dry. I wasn't finished yet, but well on my way. Unfortunately, this was to be the day that all the painful memories were to begin.

After I finished my painting project, I wanted to go bowling. I felt fine, so I decided to go. I got home about four o'clock in the morning and about four hours later I woke up. It was quite visible that the work had to be finished, so I began to get things ready for another day of painting…not knowing that there would be no more painting for me.

I walked downstairs, and as I bent over to move a baby stroller that was in my way, the pain in my back was excruciating. I fell to the floor and could not move. At first I felt that I had just turned the wrong way and at any moment the pain would simply pass. But it went on and on, and as the pain grew worse, I called for someone to help.

"Somebody, please come here. Help me!" Moments later, my husband came rushing down the stairs. "What's the matter?" he asked.

I was lying on my side with my head turned sideways as though my neck was broken. I cried, "I don't know what's wrong. I can't move."

He tried to move me, but the pain was so great I could barely stand it. Then, he called the family doctor. The doctor told him that I must have pulled a muscle, that I should rest, and he would send over some medicine for the pain. We soon found out that this medication was of no use for my problem and that the next step would most likely be to the hospital. He called the doctor back and was told to go to the hospital at once.

As the life squad came, these thoughts were running through my head: "What's wrong? It can't be all that bad. All I did was bend over. But I can't even move the pain is so bad. Will it ever stop hurting?" Sweat was pouring down me and there was so much confusion in the room. The children were crying and confused. It was all we could do to try and keep order in the house. The doctor had said to take me to the hospital where they would be ready for me, so we had to go.

When I arrived at the hospital, they gave me a shot to help ease the pain. Regrettably, instead of relief I got the most horrific feeling from the medication. I was having a violent reaction to the drug and began to vomit. They had to strap my head down because I was choking on my own vomit. Finally, my husband convinced them that I shouldn't be given that drug and that they needed to find something else.

I was moved into another hospital room and put into traction. Every move I made was extremely painful. They started me on shots that didn't make me sick and finally let me sleep. As with many patients, I grew dependent on the shots; not just to relieve the pain, but to relieve the boredom of lying in one position all of the time. I would grow so depressed that I would call for a shot…just to forget what was happening. Can you imagine how desperate one must get…to just slip away into a state that nothing matters, nothing is worth living for? For the next fourteen days I was in traction and so depressed.

With therapy, I could walk with the help of a brace. I was able to go home, but had to stay in bed sixteen hours a day for four months; lying with a towel around my neck and in a straight position. I was impossible to live with; how my family put up with me I will never know. At this point in my life I wasn't really a Christian yet, and I was still in so much pain. I was taking Empirin, Codeine, and Tylenol 3.

Eventually, I could walk a little longer each day with the help of my brace. Up until now my marriage had been nothing but sickness. I wondered, what could my husband possibly think of me? I wanted our marriage to be something beautiful and happy; not a constant state of sickness.

With that thought, a sudden sharp pain pierced my side. Oh, no! What is it this time? I cannot tell my husband. We have never had any time together without my being ill. What will he say? I had a friend take me to the doctor who said it was nothing and sent me home. The pain grew worse each day. By this time I could no longer keep control of my emotions; the pain was just too bad. Just as I began to tell my husband what was going on with me, the vomiting started. We called another doctor and I was admitted to the hospital as an emergency. I had a ruptured appendix.

When I woke up, there were tubes running out my side, my mouth, and an I.V. in my arm. I felt as if I had come back from the dead. Had I nearly met death that day? After a two-week stay, I came home, very weak and barely able to walk.

The pain started again in my abdomen. Now what? Back to the hospital for more tests. This time it was discovered that I was pregnant. I went back home again; still plagued with nausea, painful cramps, and weakness. Much to my sadness, at five and one-half months I had a miscarriage, losing the pregnancy. By now, I was so depressed I considered killing myself. Was living worth all of this?

But time does heals our wounds and eventually I was back on my feet, facing the tasks of our home and children. After everything I had been through, I looked nothing like the housewife I imagined. I was shaky and thin, losing weight, and bitter about everything and everyone. Who was I? Who had I become?

I felt anguish that our marriage was falling apart, and my sicknesses had not helped the situation at all. The one thing in life I wanted, and had found, was being torn apart by the devil…and I didn't have the faith to know that there was healing power in Jesus Christ.

Time passed and I began to gain weight and regain my health. We very much wanted the child we had lost and soon I was pregnant again. I started to gain weight, and as I reached a whopping one hundred and ninety-seven pounds, the doctor thought I might be carrying twins. On July 19, 1970, Adam Gerald Condo was born to us. He weighed eleven pounds, eleven ounces. The delivery was hard, and my husband said, as I was moved into the hall, "I'll make this up to you somehow." Besides the size of our new arrival, this was the hardest childbirth I had ever endured because I forgot to tell them about the medication I was on. The shots they gave me had no effect. Ouch!

When Adam was only two months old, I began having grand mal seizures. When the seizures became more frequent, I knew I must see a doctor. Now I know that there was one who paid the price nearly two thousand years ago for all of our sickness and pain.

> "But He was wounded for our transgressions. He was bruised for our iniquities: the chastisement of our peace was upon Him; and with His stripes we are healed." (Isaiah 53:5)

A neighbor found a doctor for me at another hospital in Cincinnati. He was one of the finest and most concerned physicians I have ever met. He was a true blessing to me, and I hope that I have enlightened his life through my faith and witness. Although this gentle doctor had my test results in front of him, he took the time to question me at length about my past life and medical history. I felt he was leading up to something, and after over an hour of talking, he asked how soon I could enter the hospital. "No, not again!" I said to myself. He calmly explained that he believed a blood clot was causing my seizures, and he must find out as soon as possible. So, once again, I entered the hospital the very next week. By this time I had begun to grow a little in faith, but still had not completely immersed myself in His grace.

All of this seemed like the same bad dream over and over again; the same entrance tests, the same questions, and the same answers. At times I felt that if they asked me one more question I would scream. I knew that if they found what they thought was there, something like a blood clot, they would perform brain surgery. This meant that all of my beautiful black hair would be shaved off...and it was down to my waist! It's strange to think that this seemed to bother me more than anything. I felt that no one cared what I was going through. They just acted as if I were getting a tooth pulled.

Later, I learned that the hospital staff and my family didn't want to act as if something serious was wrong because they didn't want to upset me. Many times, I wanted to just get up and walk out of that hospital…and walk straight into the wind. Life without Christ in it is worthless; there is no reason to live, no goal to reach, no tomorrow.

> "I have come that they might have life, and that they might have it more abundantly." (John 8:36)

Three days later, the doctor asked me to come to the hospital so we could go over the test results together. I was apprehensive and knew it was serious. When we got to the hospital, the doctor sat down and explained the test results to us.

It is in that moment that I believe I died a little that day. "The brain scan shows some damage on the right side; however, unfortunately, we cannot operate because you have a hyperthyroid. Also, you have heart disease."

This could not be happening to me. What about the children? They are too young to understand. What will happen to them? What about Adam, our baby? No, no, no, this cannot be!

This had to be the longest night I ever spent in the hospital. The sheets were cold and stiff and the night was a continual nightmare. After everything that happened to me in my youth…and now this? I hadn't been prepared even to live life, much less be prepared to die at this time. But there were to be many things in store for me; I had no idea of the Lord's plans for my life.

> "And we know that all things work together for good to them that love God, to them who are called according to his purpose." (Romans 8:28)

Over the next two years my treatment was a planned event that included the participation of the whole family. First was radioisotope treatment for thyroid; small doses at first, then up to one hundred times the normal dosage. I was sent home and came in twice a week for treatment.

I remember sitting in the room, where treatment was given, with two men who wore turtle neck sweaters. As they spoke, I realized with horror that I too might have cancer. I ran out of the office and leaned against the wall. What else? Is there more I don't know? The doctor came out and comforted me. He explained that it wasn't as bad as I thought and he told me the measures I must take to protect my family. "Mrs. Condo, there are some things that you must do after this therapy. You must not be in contact with any men because the radiation is so great that it can damage the male hormones. Also, you must use all disposable dishes, flush the water closet three times, and also use the solution that we've given you as part of your radiation treatment." Sweat poured down me, and my hands seemed like ice. Then he explained how I would take this, this monster of a solution, that makes any human a walking menace, and that I would have to live two to three weeks in our basement…away from my family…away from my baby.

There were times I could hear Adam crying and no one was tending to him. The last straw was when I heard a thump, then his loud screams. Did he fall on his head? Was he all right? I yelled, "Would someone please get him!" It seemed that no one could hear me. Finally, someone rescued him. If it hadn't been for my daughters, I don't know what I would have done through everything going on. They helped when there was no one else to turn to.

Finally, the treatment was finished and I could return to living with my family. At this time I was taking anticonvulsants, Amoxicillin, a thyroid pill, along with some other medications.

Regrettably, not long after the treatment was completed, the pain began throbbing in my head so bad that I couldn't eat or sleep. Ultimately, I fell into a sleep that no one could wake me from. It was back to the hospital and back to the lengthy entrance tests again. This time I was so sick I just told them to find my file. I couldn't, and wouldn't, be able to answer their questions. The pain had severely increased. I remembered that several days earlier I noticed numbness in my leg, so now even more tests were taken to see if there was a brain tumor present. I was given shots to kill the pain, but I slept even without them.

In the haze, there was something about "injecting into the main vein in the throat and the vein should close after pressure." There was an ice pack placed on my neck and the staff started to move me into the hall. All of a sudden, the ice pack fell off. There were doctors running all around me. "What is wrong?" They act like something is wrong!

The next day I realized that there was a blood clot the size of a softball in my throat. It took a week for this to dissolve. Here again, I could have died, but the Lord had His hand on me. Many who came to visit me thought I would never make it. I see those same people now, and they can hardly believe the miracles the Lord worked in my life. I was on over one hundred and fifty pills a week at that time.

The test results showed more damage had been done to my brain. I was having more seizures than I even realized…but the drugs covered them up. My medication was increased once again and I left the hospital hoping never to return. Of course, this was not to be. Rheumatic heart disease had caused damage to my heart valves and I was left with perforations to the heart. My blood was filled with streptococcus and the damage to my brain was determined to have been caused by encephalitis.

Our two years of marriage had been nothing but illness and there seemed to be no end in sight. Everything was going wrong. Two years of never knowing what would happen next; whether I would be in or out of the hospital, never knowing if I would even live, let alone be free from pain and able to function.

Again, I woke up to intense pain. Again, we called the doctor, and again I was admitted back into the hospital. This time, however, the nerves in my back had been attacked by the seizures and I was put into traction. My oldest daughters had missed so much school because of helping at home that they could not keep up with their studies. At this point, I was put on more medication, told to purchase traction equipment, and to come to the hospital every single day for therapy.

We didn't have any money for the equipment, and my husband was already working additional hours just to meet the every day living expenses of our family. I would lie in bed, wondering when it will all end. Where were the friends who used to visit me? Had they given up on me?

Much to my surprise, just a few short days after I had these thoughts, we received an envelope in the mail with enough money for us to purchase the traction equipment. There was no name on the envelope. We realized it was from one of God's angels. Perhaps, the gift came from one of those friends I wondered about; showing up as one of God's angels.

Soon after this event, two women came to visit me. They told me some of the truth about the healing power of Jesus; how by His stripes we are healed, and for the first time I felt hope. I asked them to return and then drifted off to sleep. They came again, and prayed in a way like I had never heard before. There was so much confusion with children crying that it was hard to concentrate on the message. They asked me if I would come to one of their homes for prayer for my healing. I said I would go, but wasn't sure I had the faith. All of this was new to me. But I was having trouble with elimination, was going blind in my left eye, and I knew that I was dying, so I agreed to go. I didn't want to die. I was desperate to live.

All the things of my past went through my mind like a high-speed movie; misery, sin, and hate. I confessed all of these things openly to the Lord in front of people I didn't even know. They began to sing, and it sounded as if the angels were singing. Someone said, "We don't need to lay hands on her; she's accepting her healing."

I fell on my hands and knees and cried out, "Lord, I'm broken, please take this all away from me. I can't stand it any longer."

I saw a tower spinning in clouds, higher and higher. I had never before had a vision. The tower was light pink with gold carving on the top.

> "The Lord is my rock and my fortress, and my deliverer; my God, is my rock, in whom I take refuge. He is my shield and the horn of my salvation, my stronghold." (Psalm 18:2)

I felt I was resting my head on Jesus' knee, and he was smoothing the hair back on my forehead. When I got up from the floor, I knew I was healed and that I needed no more medication. There was no blurred vision, no pain, no doubt. Jesus had done it all.

What seemed just a short time to me had been four hours. Four hours of crying, laughing, and praising the Lord. The nurse, a good friend of mine, who took me, could hardly believe it, and we often laugh about it now. Even though she believed enough to bring me to the prayer meeting, it still took her about two weeks before she was convinced that I was completely healed.

I knew I was healed. When my husband came home, I was washing down the walls in the living room. He was shocked. For several weeks he went around expecting me to fall into his arms with a seizure; since I had stopped all of my medication. I didn't have to wear glasses anymore either!

I was examined by the doctor at the hospital and was told that I was in perfect health. A metabolism test showed that I had perfect metabolism...and no one has perfect metabolism. I felt so good that I even had my portrait taken. The girl in the studio noticed that my pictures showed a glow all over my face.

When I asked my husband what he thought of all of this, he said, "If you had died before, I would have gotten over it. But if you die now, I will continue your steps in faith. I will make sure everybody knows that because of your love and faith in Jesus Christ, you made the choice not to continue with your medicine. I don't know what you have, but it's beautiful." He followed me around for weeks, with his arms reached out, expecting to catch me in a seizure.

With all of the medical expenses piling up, we soon fell behind in our house payments, but I was not worried about our future. I simply said, "Don't worry. Jesus will take care of us." I began praying.

On the day before the foreclosure, a friend came forward and loaned us the money to bring our payments up to date. My husband was amazed at this new development. I remember that I wanted him to know how beautiful it is to be loved and cared for by the Father. But I didn't want to push him.

When we went to bed, I asked, "Do you mind if I pray?" My husband answered, "No, but it sure will be different." My eyes filled with tears. The only prayer I could think of was my childhood prayer.

Childhood Prayer

"Now I lay us down to sleep,
I pray the Lord our souls to keep.
If we should die before we wake,
Our souls to heaven I pray you take."

Then we fell asleep.

Chapter 2
I'll Bring it to You

I studied what the encyclopedia said about the Bible, and then I read the Bible at length over the next eight days. I wanted to know what had happened to me, how it had happened, and much, much more. I read about prayer and fasting and how that would get me closer to God. With this new knowledge, I told my husband that I needed to go to a pasture to fast and pray so I could better understand what all of this meant. He said, "Go, if you must. I understand."

If I must, I will go. After only a short time I knew, more than ever before, that I had to have supper and fellowship with the Lord.

I approached one of my good friends, Mary, a woman who took me to the prayer meetings many times, about the pasture behind her home. I asked her if I could use the pasture for my plan. She got permission from her husband for me to go and I was ready to start my journey.

I took a sleeping bag and a small portion of bread and wine for communion. Rain was threatening, but I claimed that I would not get wet because I believed He would keep me dry. I was still so caught up in what the Lord had already done in healing me that I had no worry about the weather.

I prayed and rested throughout the night; receiving the baptism in the Holy Spirit and the gifts of the Spirit. In the morning, a flock of blackbirds flew into the tree above me. After resting on the branches for a while, they flew down to the ground, walking around me and up onto my sleeping bag. The cattle had not come near me all night, although I knew my resting place was their favorite resting place, too. I was remarkably aware of all my surroundings and grateful for the wondrous blessings bestowed upon me. I felt a sense of calm around me. I knew everything was going to be okay.

My surroundings were beautiful and peaceful. Then, all at once, the flock of birds flew away. As I watched the birds make their sudden departure, I realized that it was time for me to leave.

As I suspected, it rained up until about four in the morning, and in the early light, I watched as the raindrops splashed down onto the blades of green grass. What I didn't entirely understand was why no rain had fallen on me. I picked up my belongings, left the field, and headed straight toward my friend's house to show her my revelation. I said, "Feel this sleeping bag, Mary. It is dry!"

I knew that the power of the Holy Spirit would lead me and teach me all things. But the Comforter, who is the Holy Ghost, whom the Father will send in My name, the following message:

> "He shall teach you all things, and bring all things to your remembrance, whatsoever I have said unto you." (John 14:26)

A week later I made some notes about my experience:

> "August 28, 1971. It has been a week since I received the Holy Spirit. Since then, I attest that everything is from the Lord. I don't take medicine anymore, I sleep well, I love well, and I pray unbelievably for my life. I worry not for anything. I study enough to do whatever I must do."

> "August 29. Today I had a chance to witness my blessings to several people, and to realize what I never really understood before. I will need no more doctors. I will lose faith only if I quit fighting the devil and pray I am truly not of this world as of now. My spirit was so heavy, but I feel I am only walking among it. I have no fear, no want, and no hunger."

> "August 30. Today I talked to a lifetime friend who needs Christ. How to tell her and her husband? Always before, I tried to impress the doctrines of the church, but now only the faith. The temple is truly within yourself."

The notes ended, but Christ kept right on in my life. His love is more than anyone can understand, for when He comes and fills you, you want so much to tell the world. All of the lonely people, just starving for the love of Jesus Christ.

"Oh, Father, I am so unworthy of your grace and love.
I humble myself and offer myself as a willing vessel.
Do not my eyes fill with tears
As the world's problems fall upon my ears?
My heart cries out with a beat,
Oh Lord, let them salvation meet.
There are times faces look as if they are dead
Knowing not what life is, they just sin instead."

Praying became one of the most important things in life to me. At this time Adam began pulling off his glasses. Until now we couldn't get them off of him. Mary and I prayed for Adam's healing. I called the doctor to ask why Adam would not keep his glasses on. He said there might be a change in his sight or maybe he needs stronger glasses.

"Then Jesus went thence, and departed into the coasts of Tyre and Sidon. And, behold, a woman of Canaan came out of the same coasts, and cried unto him, saying, 'Have mercy on me, O Lord, thou son of David; my daughter is grievously vexed with a devil.'"

"But he answered her not a word. And his disciples came and besought him, saying, 'Send her away: for she crieth after us.' But he answered and said, 'I am not sent but unto the lost sheep of the house of Israel.'"

"Then came she and worshipped him, saying, 'Lord, help me.' But he answered and said, 'It is not meant to take the children's bread, and to cast it to dogs.'"

"And she said, 'Truth, Lord: yet the dogs eat of the crumbs which fall from their masters' table.'"

"Then Jesus answered and said unto her, 'O woman, great is thy faith; be it unto thee even as thou wilt.' And her daughter was made whole from that very hour." (Matthew 15:21-28)

Christ came so greater miracles could be done in His name. I pray now, one hundred percent of the time in my life. From then on, I expect a miracle and it comes.

Chapter 3
Adam's Miracle

One Friday morning, I took Adam to the hospital clinic. The eye doctor examined him; then called in another doctor to confirm that Adam no longer needed glasses. No, he sure didn't! Praise God!

When we got home, I explained everything to my husband; the scriptures of faith, belief, and expecting a miracle meant more to me than ever before. How, by His stripes, Adam's eyes were healed. Unfortunately, he had not shared my personal experiences with the Lord and thought that I was getting ridiculous. Many problems arose for us because of our differences in faith. This didn't stop me though.

I remember reading in the Bible that through a woman's faith a man will come into God. Of course, there were times when it was extremely hard for me to rely on that promise. It isn't easy to just lie and pray, believing this is true, when you try to explain something so super-natural.

When you try to explain how your code of conduct has changed, you just can't sit at parties and watch men and women rubbing all over each other. People just couldn't understand how I could have changed so much. They didn't see how the Holy Spirit does such unbelievable things in one's life. So many times, out of frustration, I wanted to tell those who judged my beliefs to just shut up, but I knew if I did my witness would not be of the Lord.

The Spirit began opening even more doors for me as I prayed. I remember the strong impression that I was going to be in a serious car accident with a close friend of mine. Then, just three days later, as we traveled down the highway, I quickly covered Adam with my body, just moments before the crash. The car was completely totaled; a smashed windshield, buckled doors, and the undercarriage resting on the road. Luckily, no one was hurt. The driver, my dearest friend, was amazed...and so was I. For me, this was one more confirmation of His protection over my life. God had shown me, in a material way, His guidance. I now know, without any doubt, that praying constantly is extremely important.

Chapter 4
And Who is Your Friend?

Every day the Lord begins with a new song. There is one I will never forget…and neither will my friend, Sally. We had been close friends for about ten years, and we knew everything good and bad about each other.

Sally, at this time in her life, was having marital problems. She had six children, along with her husband, Don, and she was just miserable. She called, crying and asking, "What am I going to do with him?"

Sally had never heard me talk the way I did to her before that phone call. The advice I was about to give her was not what I had said in previous conversations.

We had discussed my healing, but she didn't believe that God had created all of my healing, so to put her husband in the Lord's hands meant even less to her. We agreed to meet at the local Frisch's restaurant where she informed me, "You just don't understand me anymore."

As I began to cry, I told her that I loved and understood more now about love and life than I ever did before. As tears ran down both of our faces, she started to see something different. I agreed to come to their home, so the three of us could sit down and talk. I knew that Don would say he didn't want any of that religious talk, but at the time all I could remember was to *let my light shine*.

A neighbor came over to the house, holding a can of beer in his hand. All of us started to talk about what was going on, and Don laughed because he had known me to talk about the Lord before. He made fun of me for my beliefs, but that still didn't stop me from shining my light. God was in my heart, and I knew it. Jesus lived and died for me.

As the evening went on, that can of beer was replaced with a Coke and cursing changed to questions about Jesus. The Holy Spirit led the conversation. I had always worn heavy glasses to read, but in that moment I could read the Bible without my glasses on. No matter how far they pushed it from me, I could still read it; even across the room. "You've memorized it," they declared.

After much praying and reading of the scriptures, Sally accepted Jesus as her Savior. Then her husband, Don, began to cry.

Soon after, I remember calling one day and asking, "Don, has the Lord put conviction upon your heart yet?" He replied, "I don't know, but I keep crying." I yelled, "Praise the Lord, Don, you are on your way up the mount!"

Don didn't understand why, but with every tear he felt cleaner and closer to Jesus. Oh, glory to God. For these tears He died. The whole family was saved. Don witnessed to truck drivers he knew, while Sally raised her children in the way of the Lord so that they, too, would not depart from Him.

Chapter 5
Come Unto Me

By this time, all I wanted to do was work for the Lord. If I couldn't drive, I would walk. From the looks of the neighborhood, and with all the drugs running wild on the streets and in the schools, the young teenagers needed Christ more and more each day.

This is when the burden of my heart began; my own little mission field where I, for the next few years, would preach the saving grace of our Lord Jesus Christ. I might preach it in different ways, but always with the same love; yesterday, today, and tomorrow...for He must manifest Himself through me. There is a feeling like no other, when a child of the world puts on the full armor of God. We have seen so many cry out to the Lord, as they kneeled at the altar, humbling themselves in front of man and God, knowing that the devil is right outside the door waiting to devour them.

My husband and I decided to start a bus ministry. We called day in and day out in search of new riders to take to church. So far, we had seventeen filling the seats; Sally's family and ours was all that we had at the time, but we didn't stop there. Our next step was to find children in the neighborhood to join.

In order for me to reach the teenagers in the neighborhood, I would have to begin with one child at a time; choosing the meanest one in the group. My hope was that I would gain the trust of others who followed him. His parents agreed that he needed religion, and said that I could talk to him until a fight came on television.

I told this boy the story of Jesus and His love for him. He knew that I really meant what I said, and that I had made a commitment. I explained how I believed that he was a boy God could use. In that moment, our friendship began, and he became our first of many new bus riders. Can you believe it? The fight on television was delayed for forty-five minutes. Praise God. He gave me the time I needed to get His work started.

Drugs are one of the devil's most powerful tools. It is one thing to fight the devil, but fighting the devil's drugs is out and out combat. We watched as so many that knelt at the altar, crying out to God, went back on the streets to be devoured once again by this tool of the devil.

As we continued our search to help, we learned that drugs were dealt at the shopping center. So off I went; handing out tracts and Bibles. After talking to these young people, I often invited some of them to my home. You probably think I was crazy for opening my home, which this would be dangerous, but man can kill only the flesh; only the Lord can make judgment upon you. When you walk in the Spirit, there is no fear.

On one of our trips to the shopping center, I met a young boy who did everything the devil had to offer. He painted his body like Alice Cooper, did drugs, and got into trouble. However, this one wanted something better in life. He wanted a new beginning.

After this boy came home with us one evening, he decided to attend church. Soon afterward, he made a commitment to Christ. He changed. His beliefs changed, his actions changed, and even his dirty pants were changed...into dress pants. He had lost his parents when he was only fourteen and had been looking for love ever since. Jesus was the real love this boy wanted...and needed.

He moved on, as so many have in those past years, to a very fulfilling life. He, like many others, was a blessing while he was with us. At the altar he poured out his problems to Jesus, crying and asking forgiveness.

Chapter 6
Where Will It All Come From?

On weekends, our little Mt. Airy home became a regular gathering place for all kinds of teenagers. Food became a hefty expense, but we were determined to make a difference in the lives of these children. Everyone who came to our home knew there was love, and I guess some came in the beginning just to eat the offerings we made. Here we were open and free in clean laughter. Those who came knew they could leave their personal hell outside the door; they could come in and receive a touch from the Master.

Between my home, family, church, babysitting, and witnessing, I started doing too much. I grew very nervous, knowing that I couldn't keep up this pace. "Lord, let me know Thy will. There is so much to be done." No one even seemed to care how the youngsters survived in the filth that was all around them. My heart cried out for them. It was really the love that my Jesus gave to me that made the change.

On Easter Sunday the Lord gave me the privilege of meeting a young girl. She was standing at the altar. She told me she had tried to physically harm her mother and that she was on a pass from a mental hospital. She asked me if I would come to see her…and I did.

There, I found men and women ranging from thirteen to eighty years of age. Some of the young patients were on drugs; just minutes away from the schools or streets where they were introduced to them. Some parents felt they had no other choice but to commit them for their own safety. All I could do was pray. What is going to happen to this sick, devil-infested world? Some of the children were permanently damaged from LSD; suffering from the flashbacks.

The day that I visited her, I came home sick.

My husband said, "If visiting these kids is going to upset you this much, you'll have to stop going there." Being the willful woman I was, I just couldn't leave things the way they were. To tell the story of Jesus and His love seemed more important than ever now. This is a love so deep that you cry for the souls of others. The Lord exposed me to so much in such a short amount of time.

I talked to so many of the patients at this hospital, and I would come home and pray for them for hours, for there was no other way I could help. I was told I could visit the one girl, but not to try "my religion" on anyone else. Even with this warning, I believed that the Lord had arranged for me to witness there and I would do it until I was told to leave. Expecting to be asked to leave anytime, I thanked God each time I was permitted another visit.

During one of my visits, I met a tall, beautiful, thirteen-year-old girl who was addicted to *soapers* (downers). She had lived an unhappy childhood and was cold and angry with everyone and everything. She was given a Living Bible from someone and we would sit and talk about her learning. Then, as if a switch was turned, she would get up suddenly and walk away with an older man. As strange as it might sound, here, people of all ages and gender were mixed together.

Before she left, I told her that if she wanted to call me, I was more than happy to talk with her. I gave her my phone number and off she went.

Finally, one day she called and asked me to come and pray with her. I went, but was refused admittance. Meanwhile, without anyone knowing, she slipped down the back steps and called to me. Word had gotten out that somebody had been preaching salvation and that they must be stopped. Until the person or their phone number was found, the elevator was locked and all passes had to be issued.

She told me she was getting more "junk" there, in the hospital, than she did on the streets. She was so mixed up and confused and she didn't know if she could stay off the stuff. Just then her doctor walked up and loudly ordered me into his office.

I acknowledged my faith in Jesus to him and told him I was only trying to help. The girl's father was in the hallway, waiting, because she refused to see him or the rest of her family. The girl announced that she would not eat, talk, or cooperate in any way if she couldn't talk directly to me. The doctor told the family he didn't want religion involved in his daughter's case. With her family receiving this new information, they had to come to some sort of decision. Thank God, she didn't stay there long.

Soon after she left the hospital, she called me at my home. Her parents agreed that she could visit church with us as long as she also went to Mass. The Lord touched her and answered her cry for help. I was filled with joy to see the miracles of faith.

One sunny day, all of us went to Kings Island, an amusement park located in Ohio. Much to our dismay, she left us there. That evening she called and said she was very sorry for leaving. I thought she needed to realize her responsibility toward others so I didn't call her back.

You can't ever underestimate a teenager in need. That following Sunday, into the service she came; dressed in a halter top and low boy jeans. She had hitchhiked ten miles to come to church that day. I wondered what everyone would think, but the scripture in James came to mind.

> "For is there come unto your assembly a man with a gold ring, in goodly apparel, and there come in also a poor man in vile raiment; And ye have respect to him that weareth the gay clothing, and say unto him, Sit thou here in a good place and say to the poor, Stand thou there, or sit here under my foot-stool: Are ye not then partial in yourselves, and are become judges of evil thoughts?" (James 2:2-4)

How could I expect her to know any better; she was completely lost. She began to breakdown and cry; then with my arms around her, I started to cry, too. God again gave me the privilege to lead one such as this to the feet of Christ. Between telephone conversations and continual prayer, this girl still calls to tell me, "Mrs. Condo, I'm still straight." I find her more beautiful than ever before because of her experience with Christ. Glory to God. I know that through His perfect timing, He chose me to be His servant.

Chapter 7
Donuts

Things happened which were almost hard to believe; the doughnuts, for instance. We needed some food for the families to eat on our bus route. One Saturday, when my husband and I were eating at a nearby doughnut shop, I said, "I wonder what they do with their leftover doughnuts."

I don't know what they did with them before, but for the next three months, the bus riders had doughnuts every Sunday on the way to church. Every time someone asked me what we had to eat, I handed them a doughnut. I had asked the Lord, if possible, to let us have some doughnuts because He knew the kids didn't have any breakfast. We received more than a hundred dozen a week. Now that is a lot of donuts! When you ask, expect a miracle.

Even with the doughnuts, our food bill had gotten way out of control. My husband asked, "What are we going to do?" I knew all we had to do was ask and He would answer.

"Ask, and it shall be given; see and ye shall find; knock and it shall be opened unto you." (Matthew 7:7)

That very same day, a lady phoned me and asked if I would tell her prayer group about the teenagers and their needs. (I say "tell" because I am not a speaker). That day it had snowed about an inch, rained, and then froze. We slid there instead of driving.

Because of the bad weather, only six people from the group came. As I told of the struggles against the devil and the need to keep the youngsters fed, the Spirit moved.

I came home with meat, groceries, and eleven dollars. My husband wanted to know what I had told them. "All I told them was what was going on here at our house. You asked how we were going to feed God's children and He answered you. Praise God!"

Even with all the help we received, we were still going through tons of food. Every Sunday, after church services, we would eat an old-fashioned breakfast. Sometimes there were twelve to eighteen kids to feed. Each time we went through four dozen eggs, three pounds of bacon, three gallons of milk, and countless loaves of bread.

All of the children knew that the head of the house always ate first. They knew the rules and stayed respectful to our expectations.

On weekends, the kids could drink as many as sixteen cartons of soft drinks; then followed the grill and five pounds of hotdogs. The Lord helped.

Many of the children came just for the food, and we knew this, but through the stomach to their hearts just happened to be the way the Lord worked. We had old-time religion and good food to go with it.

God just kept sending children for me to care for during the week to meet the need we had for money. Babysitting was one way we were able to keep up with all the food expense and we were thankful.

All was not in vain, for we became aware of the love Christ placed in our hearts. Though there is sometimes confusion in our home, the joy that fills our souls is worth every headache. It cost as much as fifty-five dollars a week for us to feed our drop-ins, and I wouldn't change what we gave for a minute.

One Christmas we wanted to buy gifts for all of the teenagers. Now this was going to be difficult considering we had seven children of our own to tend to. We decided that we would charge the presents on our good old Sears charge card.

Many needed clothing, coats, and winter gloves for their cold hands. Winter can be cruel to the body, and when I see a young boy rubbing his hands together to keep warm, it does something to me. The scene brings back memories of my childhood; me trying to keep warm during the cold winters. The Lord provided and they all had a nice Christmas.

The day after Christmas I received checks totaling fifty dollars, with a note attached, requesting that I use the money for the kids.

Praise the Lord! This is God and faith working together. If I have learned one thing, it is to depend upon the Lord. He never lets me down and He will never let you down, either. Praise God.

With the donations of doughnuts and gifts from others whose hearts the Lord had touched, our work with teenagers went on.

At this time, my husband and I felt that the Lord wanted us to start a full-time ministry with teenagers. Sometimes we thought we knew what the Lord wanted us to do, and we rushed right into the idea before giving it some thought. We prayed and talked for endless hours about what to do. Was God really moving us into the position that we might do his work full-time?

"For which of you, intending to build a tower, sitteth not down first, and counteth the cost, whether he have sufficient to finish it?" (Luke 14:28)

Chapter 8
Where to Go

I prayed, Lord, if this is what you want, please let my husband make this decision. Within a very short period of time, that is exactly what happened. My husband made the decision for us. He said he thought we should get ourselves in a position to move where we could hold the fellowship for the youth…a place where we could make a bigger difference We wondered, as many people do, is this what God really wants from us? Are we in His will? Several things confirmed that we were walking closer to His direction so we went with it.

One confirmation arrived at about two o'clock in the morning, when a boy telephoned our home. "Mrs. Condo, can I come over and talk with you? I have had a really bad trip. Please can I come over?" This boy was known for his use of acid and he desperately needed our help.

My husband and I had made a commitment to never turn anyone away, and this wouldn't be the case now. In fact, we made ourselves available twenty-four hours a day, seven days a week. Many times, we wondered if we were just a place for kids to munch out, or if we were really servants of the Master. Our answer came as we sat and prayed with this boy, one of the lost ones, much in need of a touch from the Master.

He poured his heart out to us; upset that his family was always fighting. He went on to say that they never attended church and there really was no genuine, real love being shown. To top it all off, he had car problems and no way to fix them.

My husband prayed with the boy until four o'clock in the morning. He always prayed better than me; probably because he was the head of the house. I felt the joy of the Lord, so present and strong.

If you ever want to feel like you just won a million dollars, just lead someone to the Lord.

The boy left us that same morning, but he called the very next day...extremely excited about the changes he was experiencing. The changes started with his grandparents, making it clear to the family that there will be no more fighting; then something pushed him to go out and check one of his hub caps. Much to his surprise, the hub cap was his car trouble...and he thought he had transmission troubles.

I praise God for the moving of His Spirit. There is no greater joy. "I am just a vessel, Lord, use me as You will. Because I was nothing until You took me and filled me with Holy Spirit."

As I tried to express myself, the Holy Spirit brought tears to my eyes. I pray, "Lord, let me never be of the world, only in it, and at Thy service. Thank you, Jesus. Keep me humble."

"Glory to the Son of God," as the words touched my heart, I was filled to overflowing. "Lord, place me in Your will. One of God's children went on his way now with a touch from the hand of my Jesus."

Later, when I visited the boy in the hospital, he said to a friend, "Listen to this lady. I know she is right...now."

Aside from this boy, and everyone and everything that required our attention, being a housewife meant to clean, clean, clean, and cook, cook, cook. The young people never failed to amaze me either. I remember one weekend we had kids in our home from Friday through Sunday. Wet towels, dirty dishes, and soiled clothes were all over the place. It was all too much for me to keep clean. I needed some help.

Even with all of the mess surrounding our home at the time, we still decided to go to church that Sunday night. Unfortunately, none of the young people would go with us. However, what we didn't realize at the time was that they had a plan. When we got home, we found that everything was clean; from dishes to the walls...spotless.

All I could do was cry. I think my husband had to hold a tear or two back, too. The kids just stood there and smiled; love radiating from their faces like angels. Love overcometh all. These moments are the ones I always cherish. By this time, we were already talking about the possibility of an open house for these teens. This only confirmed our idea.

One night a friend asked me to visit a church in Dayton where the gifts of spirit were in operation. She knew the burden on my heart and wanted to help me in some way. For the most part, I went so I could pray in a church where no one knew me but the Master. During the service there was a call for prayer, but I felt that if the Lord had a word for me, he would come to me. I sat there with my eyes closed and my hands raised; just then the evangelist grabbed my hand. I knew my request to the Lord was granted. This was the prophecy.

"You have sought so much and gotten so little. I'm not speaking of the worldly possessions, but I'm speaking of life in general. You've sought for some great things in life, but ended up with one pressure after another that you're not able to solve. But you know, tonight the Lord is going to start giving you some directions in your life. Yes, He knows the way out of that wilderness that you're in right now."

"Now I see the pull that's been pulling you back and forth between grabbing onto the things God's given you and the pull that's trying to take you the other way. Things were a lot easier before you started serving the Lord, in the natural, but you have to sit down now and count the cost. The Bible says that before a man builds a house, does he not sit down and count the cost to see if he can afford the price of it. A lot of things happen to see if you're going to be able to go on to the deeper meanings of God; like praying for the sick and caring for the lost, but this other side of your life that does not under-stand why you can change and be like you are, all of a sudden, when you used to be so different. You used to be so much fun in the natural and you're getting grounded in that religion. God's going to give you some answers."

"Sister, you have a real faith and that's one thing that helps you...actually, it is the only thing that brought you through. Tonight God is going to touch your body. You're going to feel a miracle in your nerves. I don't understand, but I see God has his hand on you. I also see you departing from some things you have been holding on to. I am not talking about the world now, but religious things, spiritual things. He's trying to lead you out into a greater realm of the Spirit. A lot of things you don't understand right now. You have been through one confusing tragedy after another, not because you wanted it, but because this is the kind of thing that you had to come through."

"God said to tell you you're going to start seeing your way out of this trouble. You've wondered how this thing was going to work out because it does involve someone else. If you will let the Lord work it out, you will be happy about it; however, if you do what you think, or what some other people think, you're going to be miserable. The Lord saved you and filled you, He gave you promises of what He was going to do with somebody very close to you, and they haven't been fulfilled yet, but God does not lie."

"There is going to be a change; a miracle in the life of this one you have been praying for. You're going to see it happen very soon. God, touch this precious woman."

Chapter 9
He Will Listen

The work of a housewife of God goes on and on. There were so many young people to help. There were Gus's, Dave's, Bruce's, Pat's, Kevin's, and Roger's. There were Charles's, Mike's, Tom's, Van's, Lee's, Kim's, Terry's, and Kathy's. You name it, they were there. I would think, "If only you would let Him use you, let Him show you how to love."

One of the boys had come to our home for almost six months before he began to respond to this message. He finally asked if he could attend church with us on Sunday. Until now, he mostly used our home for a crash pad (a place to stay until the drugs wore off). Many of our friends felt we were wrong to allow such kids into our home, but the Lord always ate with sinners and how much greater He is than we are. That following Sunday, the boy attended our church.

As the pastor asked anyone to stand who felt as if they were not living up to God's will, if they dishonored their parents in some way, or if they needed a change to get things straight, the boy stood. I watched in amazement as he stood quietly with his head hung low.

Although this isn't my first time watching this transformation, I cry every time I see one happen. Some kids don't make it all the way, but when they meet Jesus, they never forget the experience. I know how hard it is for these kids to publicly acknowledge Christ and they make Him so proud.

Later that day, when we got home from church, we talked about his problem. What was he going to do...his grades were so behind what he needed to pass and exams were coming up soon? Since my husband was so much better at math, I turned the problem over to him. With him leading, we worked all day and night until it was time for bed. The only thing we could do was call the school and ask if they would give him extra time to catch up on his work. In order for us to make the call, there was one more commitment the boy had to make. He must tell the school that he was on drugs.

He went to his counselor and explained his situation. He couldn't have done this if he didn't know Christ was the answer. No one knew he was on drugs. No one was pressuring him to tell his counselor, but he knew he must come clean in order to get the help he needed.

When his counselor heard him confess his addiction, and how he wanted another chance to pass, she knew he was on the up and up. "Please call Mrs. Condo," he pleaded. "She can explain better than I can what has happened to me."

The counselor called and explained what this boy had told her. I knew the Lord had moved as only He could. To get caught is one thing, but to turn yourself in is something else altogether. The school knew nothing of this boy. As we talked, I knew the Lord had the situation all taken care of. He was given a private tutor two days a week and time and hard work would begin to heal his future. She asked me how many other boys I knew who were on drugs from their school. I told her, "I am sorry, but until they are ready to come forward and tell you, they are not ready to kick their habit." She wanted to know if I worked with any agency, like Talbert House. I told her, "No, just with Jesus." I know He is all I need, for it is not I who has done this but Jesus through me.

She couldn't get over the transformation of this boy. He had commented, "As long as I have this Bible in my pocket, I'll make it."

But the devil was sure to try and break this new Christian at any cost. There were no fellow Christians to help guide him, which is what makes it so hard for these new babes in Christ. Their family and friends make fun of them so they are basically on their own to move forward with Christ. It's so bad that his friends even threatened to hold him down and force drugs on him. They are like a twig in a hailstorm.

The streets were a personal hell for these kids. They come in at ten in the morning asking about the plan of salvation. With tears in their eyes, they wonder just what they are going to do. They see the peace and want to taste it.

There were more of them than I could count; some who came in the early morning hours and others late into the evening. I got so familiar with the routine that I could tell when someone wanted to talk because they lingered well after the others had gone. That is when I could feel the Spirit of God move. From that moment on, things would drop right in line.

There was one night I wish you could have seen the eight boys in our front yard; all of them holding hands in friendship and beginning to understand the word of God. I watched as they prayed together. All had past lives that seemed out of the movie *The Cross and the Switchblade*. Their loyalty was unbelievable. One of the boys, Jack, who was the toughest one around, said, "Anyone who doesn't go by the rules around here will hear from me."

Jack had bleached-blond hair and horseshoe heels. Heels, that when he fought, left an imprint on his opponent's face. He walked around like he wanted to take on the whole world. He had a chain hanging from his waist that could cut a face open in seconds.

All of this hate he held. How could anyone have been hurt so badly? I, of all people, should know and understand, for that same cruelty had happened to me. He saw God in our home and he knew we loved him and the others. The Lord sets no limits to the love he puts in your heart.

So many times, I would sit on the porch and wonder what was going to happen to this lost generation. They drive like crazy, without even knowing where they are going. Some are rushing up the road to the next hit of their favorite drug or making their next score. You might not think drugs and pot would be so open in a neighborhood, but they are all around us.

If you are a parent, you might even be surprised to find out that your own child has tried the stuff. Don't kid yourself. Smoking pot is used as openly as drinking was when you and I were teenagers. There is a reason why I say you won't know…because mine tried it, too. Having a mother in the position I'm in doesn't help when you're a teenager. Just ask one of my kids. You try and tell them and wonder if you are doing a good job, but you never really know. All you can do is pray and put them in the Lord's hands.

Chapter 10
He Listened and Knew

No matter what happened, I heard about it some way. I think it was because I always tried to keep my mouth shut and listen. Sometimes I would slip up, but it always cost me when I did. Of course, you can't make too many of these mistakes. When there is trouble in the group, you have to tend to the issue.

There was only one boy I actually had to tell to leave and not come back. His disruption to the group couldn't be tolerated any longer. When one hinders the moving of the Spirit, that person must go for the sake of the others. For you don't ever encourage the devil.

There were a lot of problems we had to deal with in and outside of the group. Aside from the troubled children needing our help, there were parents who resented us talking to their children. Another issue was smoking. All of the kids smoked and I knew in my heart that it was wrong. How could I tell them that they couldn't smoke? Then, just as if the Lord had heard my thoughts, He took care of this delicate issue. Adam became allergic to smoke. Although this wasn't good for Adam, it did correct the problem. When I explained why they couldn't smoke in the house, they understood completely. Praise the Lord!

It was around this time that Jack, who I mentioned earlier, came to be a steady visitor at our home. What a privilege it is to lead a child to the Master.

Jack was on the streets at the young age of fourteen years old. He was very angry with God and man. I knew the need to be loved was the only thing that attracted such a boy to us. At first he came just for a place to eat. After all, where else was he going to go? His parents had given up on him...even telling him to leave. But God hadn't given up on him.

When we first met Jack we knew that he learned what he knew by living on the streets. He knew all the people and places to go to get a fix. He started on pills and ended up on acid; a devil-inspired drug. Jack wrote this during one of his acid trips:

"Where am I? What am I doing? Where am I going? Where should I go? Why am I here on earth? What is my purpose on earth? What am I here to do? My God, am I dead?"

"I'm dead but yet my spirit still walks. I can still think, but I can't hear or smell or taste. Nobody speaks to me or even knows I'm around. I'm not walking, I'm floating. Nobody will talk to me. It's as though I'm just here to watch and observe. Should I go home? But wait, what's home? Who are my mother and father? They have no meaning to me now."

"Everything seems to pass through me. I have no feeling. Nothing can hurt or touch them. I am God!!! I have to tell somebody this."

"But nobody talks to me. Nobody hears me. I am so lonely. I have to get somebody to help me. Just anybody. Please, Mister, will you stop and talk to me? He acts as if I'm not even here. I can't see my body. My body is gone."

"I am between time. I can't get out!! I am inside my brain. Something, somebody has to destroy me. My God, destroy me. I hate you, destroy me!!!! I can't see!!! Help me!!!"

"This is the most horrifying and lone feeling you can get!!!"

Jack got so involved that he had to sell drugs just to feed his habit. His nickname was Speed. He even had it tattooed on his arm for the world to see. He had fought his way through life and was approaching a dead-end.

Finally, Jack heard that you could get a meal and understanding from some lady at the corner of Aries and Burgess. He came, and Jesus led us the rest of the way. This is how he told it:

"I'm an ex-dope addict. I'm seventeen years old and I've lived on the streets for the past three years. I have done everything and experienced everything that the streets had to offer. I have taken dope; everything from acid and heroin to smoking pot and popping pills, such as Darvon and Librium."

"My hair used to be long and I wore earrings. I used to get into rock bands playing hard rock and I loved it. This used to be my life. Acid used to be my life. Whenever I felt down, I always turned to acid. Acid was how I lived. Acid was my religion, as you call it. Acid was my answer to everything. And a lot of people don't even know what acid is. But to me, acid was the answer. Acid was my mother, it was my father, and acid was my God."

"I've done a lot of other drugs, such as heroin and smack. I've shot speed and I've taken uppers, but I always came back to one thing... acid."

"Acid tears your body up. Acid goes in and it messes with your mind. Acid can mess up your chromosomes to where if you have a kid, he will come out deformed. I knew all of this when I first started taking acid, but at the same time I didn't care. I didn't care whether I lived or died."

"I was only fourteen and my mother had been dead for two years. To make matters worse, my dad remarried only two weeks after my mother died. He told me that he had been messing around with this woman before my mother had died. I loved my mother, and after she died and my dad told me this, I started hating the world."

"I started not to care what happened to me, not to care what happened to anybody. Acid became my God, and as far as God was concerned, I didn't care whether He came or He went. I didn't care about anything. All I wanted to do was to destroy my body. I just wanted to withdraw from the world completely."

"I live in the streets. I was fourteen when I first ran away. My dad, stepmother, and little sister started tearing down my mother's memory and I couldn't stand to be there anymore, so I ran away to Florida. I lived on the beach for a couple of weeks until I got caught and sent home. Two months later I ran away again; only to get caught in Arkansas."

"I still didn't want anything to do with my dad so I left again; getting as far as Mexico. After this, my dad told me that he didn't want anything else to do with me, that he didn't want me around the house. I was only fourteen then."

"I caught up with a couple friends who took me in, and I lived with them for about a year and a half. They were my buddies, but not really anyone who I could sit down and just really lay my problems out to. You know what I mean…someone I could tell how things were happening, how I was feeling. I could never tell them that. I was always afraid they'd make fun of me. I needed somebody that was older than me, somebody I could almost look up to as my mother."

"My friends figured I was old enough to know what I was doing. I started to indulge in sex…and I mean in all the sex perversions you can imagine. I started doing just about any ungodly act that you can think of."

"Then, finally, there was a lady who took the time to listen to me. This lady was different from most of the others. You could tell that she really cared about you. She actually sat down and listened to what was wrong. She would stop and ask me what was wrong with me whenever I looked like I was feeling sad."

"Then one day she told me about God. Now I'd heard of Him, but hadn't given Him much thought. When I was younger, I was brought up in a Baptist church, but the lessons had been forgotten. Now, this lady started telling me about God. This time, however, I looked at religion differently. I looked at church differently. And that's why, for the first time ever, I saw myself as I was. I started seeing how worthless my life was and how I had accomplished nothing. All I was doing was tearing myself up."

We knew Jack that was sleeping in a house with some friends of his; making his bed on the floor and eating any place he could find. After much discussion, telling him of what faith in God can do, he became a steady visitor at our home. Soon after, the day came when he would experience the Master and His love beyond belief.

I will never forget the first day Jack walked into our church. There are others who won't forget either, because this boy could not go unnoticed. His walk, dress, and hair showed hate for everything and everyone. As the burden of my heart grew for him, the burden was also shared by others in the church. They learned of his problem and lifted him up in support.

Jack promised not to do drugs while he was in our home, and if he did, we would not let him come into the midst of the others. He tried to keep his promise, I guess, but soon it happened...and on the very night we were going to a revival at the church. I was so busy getting the others ready that I didn't even notice that Jack was stoned. There were several boys with us that night, all addicted to drugs of some kind, and we prayed the Holy Spirit would move like a mighty wind.

I prayed, "Oh Master, please touch these lost infested ones." As the tears poured down my face and the utterance came upon me, I knew the Lord was working a miracle. As I looked over, four boys, who had always been hard and bitter, were crying. The emotion was indescribable. As the pastor gave the altar call, the boys knelt at the altar, repenting and weeping. They knew their way of life had been of the devil. As praises were sung to the Lord, His Spirit moved, and as Jack fell to the floor, he began to weep. I felt impressed to ask for deliverance and several men came to pray with Jack. Here's how he remembers that night:

> "I was tripping when I came to church. And that was the night. It had to be then, because all of that day I was tripping with acid. I started early in the morning and I tripped all day long. This time, when I took the acid, it was really a bad trip."

> "I walked into the church; still tripping and feeling very confused. I didn't really understand what the preacher was saying, but he got up and called for altar call. I went up to the altar, got down on my knees, and started crying. I was still high, but started crying like it was the end of the world."

> "I cried for about a half an hour, until this lady came up to the altar. I had a tattoo on my arm that said, 'Speed' which became visible to everyone as she raised up my shirt sleeve, asking the other people who were at the altar to pray for my deliverance from dope. First, they started rebuking the devil; then this man came up and laid the Bible on my hand."

> "When he did that, I had such a comfort in me that I'd never known before. I've committed to memory the comfort."

> "Here I was sprawled out in the middle of the altar, right in front of the whole congregation. Me, an ex-dope addict,

sprawled out in front of the organ, crying, like I was a little baby. I used to rule the streets. I used to fight for pleasure. Me! I had the reputation of a fighter and dope addict. Me! Just laying there, crying my eyes out."

"But, man, as I hit that floor, something came over me. I wasn't tripping anymore! I was perfectly sober and I knew everything that was going on around me. And I felt God touch me. And I felt this comfort in me I'd ever know."

There are several different kinds of acid; all of which are bad for you. What Jack had in his pocket was called *Window Pane*. He asked one of the boys to take it out of his pocket and place it on the altar. The miracle became even more real to these boys who knew him so well. There, on the floor, was this boy they knew as someone so tough, who was crying like a baby, but now he was a man. And as a man he had many things he would be responsible for and there would be many trials for him.

Jack received the Holy Spirit about a week after his conversion and he began praying in tongues. I remember the night he said, "It is real (Holy Spirit Baptism), and I'm not leaving the altar until I receive it." That is just what happened. He spent two hours there and came back to our home with the joy of the Lord in his heart.

A new creature is what he became...and it showed. We didn't have to tell him to cut his hair; the hunger for the Word convinced him and he did as the Master commands. First, he asked me to cut his hair and then he removed his earrings.

We had been praying over the last two years of our ministry that we would see at least one soul that we had brought to Jesus filled with the Spirit. Much to our surprise, the most unexpected one was the head of the list.

A new life was beginning for Jack and we invited him to move in with us. He had a great deal of adjusting to do; not to mention, so did we. He had never conformed to anything or anyone before so it was going to be difficult. In fact, it was hard on all of us. What was helpful is that he knew we loved him and that was the most important thing. The kind of love he got here was real. For once you experience the love of Jesus, you must pass it on. There is no other love like the love of Jesus. It is simple enough for the smallest child to understand and deep enough to satisfy adult yearnings.

Jack was an artist and he spent some of his free time drawing visions of Christ. He drew the Master with tears running down his cheeks. I asked, "Why do you see tears on the Master's face?" He would answer, "When He sees all of us junkies, He just cries."

After a long stay with us, Jack decided to enter the Marines. Before he left, he painted his vision of the face of Christ on our daughter's wall. He signed his work "Christ, not Jack." He said, "For it is Christ, not me."

The night before Jack left for the Marine Corps, he told us,

"I know I'm still a babe in Christ. I still have a lot of growing to do. Yet I know that you just can't change completely, but your thoughts can change completely overnight. I don't know what's going to happen to me, but I know that if I just keep in prayer, if I keep reading the Bible, and I have faith that my church is praying for me, I'll make it. I know that I'll grow in Christ."

"I would never have come off dope; I would never have left the streets, if you hadn't taken the time to ask me, 'What's the matter?' I wish there were more people who would go out and take the time to approach a dirty hippy, a dirty street fighter, and ask him what's wrong...someone who would sit down and tell him that Jesus loves him, someone who would take the time to listen to him."

"I just hope that when I get home from the service that I'll be able to come up to a teenager, girl or boy, even a dirty hippie, and say, 'Jesus loves you, Jesus cares' so they know that they are loved."

Chapter 11
Woman to Woman

It was about this time that a woman named Mrs. Lancomb came to visit me. That day, I had ten young children and eight teenagers. The person with her said, "I don't think she has time for this."

Mrs. Lancomb's reply was, "I think this is what she needs." They were from the Women to Women program; a program where people go into prisons and meet with inmates.

After much discussion, we decided to try the program. What I didn't know was that this also was to be a fulfillment in the work of Christ. He so often fills us for His own personal task.

You probably wonder if I am still a housewife. Yes, but only with God in my heart and soul. He will let you meet someone who no one else is able to talk to. This was the case with the inmate I met.

I'll never forget the experience. I must say, she was a beautiful person as the Lord moved in her life. She was very tall, about three months pregnant, and frightened. Of all the inmates, I sensed she would be the most opposed to my intentions. That is putting it mildly! She said, "Here I am, baby, what can you do for me?" I had to think on that statement.

I answered, "I don't know, but sit down and let's see what I can do." That began a relationship that still continues today. I grew and became even more open through the prison work that I did, and I learned more of the conditions that the inmates had to adjust to. As I talked to different women, I realized that there are some who never have a letter or any other kind of communication from the outside world. Many of them have been in prison most of their lives with little to no connection to outside those prison walls.

One female prisoner, who was serving a sentence for killing her husband, seemed to have so much peace. I asked her how she could be so peaceful and she answered, "If I hadn't accepted the Lord nine years ago, I would have killed myself." Her acceptance made me realize how fortunate we are to have the freedom to know the Lord as we do. To think that He made it possible for me to work in His plan, and with this particular one; God is her only hope in her world of hate, abuse, and sins of perversion. We cannot begin to understand her feelings, how much more the Master means to her than to many of us. I talked with her often, but still never grasping her true feelings about His holiness. She asked, "Can you get someone to write to me? I don't care who it is, anyone, just so it is a letter." You can't begin to know how many are there; crying out to you, "Write to me, please, or come and see me; your kindness would mean so much." I can't write to them all, but, Christians, they are waiting for you.

I wrote a poem for these lost souls. The ones who the Lord had put a burden on my heart.

PRISON

"Here I sit, lonely with tear,
Wanting and wanting for someone to hear.
Love is something not often I find,
Sometimes I think I'll lose my mind.
Then in a letter of some kind,
Someone said the love of Jesus is yours and mine.
Now in my cell instead of dismay,
Through Jesus Christ I've found my way."

This burden of life in prison weighed heavily on me. I learned that there were sixty inmates who never received gifts for Christmas. It troubled me, until the Lord impressed upon me to ask if I might send packages for these less fortunate prisoners. After much discussion, it was decided that packages could indeed be sent. The Lord never fails. All you need to do is give Him all the honor and glory. I got a list of items I could send and I was on my way to do more of the Lord's work.

There were twenty-four items, which would mean food for their bodies; however, they needed food for their souls, too. According to the rules of the penal system, a package can come only from someone on their mailing list. The package must be inspected at the prison and no literature can go into the prison unless it is sent directly from a bookstore. Now was the time that I needed a miracle from the Lord.

"...ye have not because ye ask not." (James 4:2)

After making several phones calls to ask if I might be able to send a Bible in each package, I was told I would be called back. Much time had passed, and then finally the phone call I was waiting for came. "Mrs. Condo, you may put a Bible in each package. Also, you may wrap the packages in holiday wrappings, if you send one to us as a sample, and we will not open the rest." Praise the Lord!

I began making calls to get the food together; twenty-four items for sixty inmates. Within two days, nearly a thousand dollars worth of food was promised. Then there were the Bibles; thirty-six dollars worth. I called Marion to help with a cash donation and she brought over a check for the whole amount.

I was so overwhelmed at what the Lord had done. It was asked in His name and for the glory of God. He hears the prayers of the inmates in the reformatory. He hears my every prayer and gives me strength to move as His servant.

Chapter 12
I Was in Prison and You Visited Me

One evening, other women in the program met at my house to pray for their inmates. It was about this time that three boys came to the door. At first, I was inclined to send them away, but then thought this might be the Lord's way of giving us an insight into the drug problems of our inmates. Just as I suspected, the evening turned out to be a blessing for each one of us.

The boys told of their outlook on drugs, why they used them, and how easy it was to get them. One of the boys used Freon; fumes from a chemical used in air conditioners. When we asked if they would pray with us, he said, "Free me from Freon." This started faith moving, the good old Pentecostal faith, and the Holy Spirit moved within us. Another fifteen-year-old knew of spiritual things, but the devil worked in him every way possible to fight the Spirit of the Lord.

The women meeting there that night were lifted, and each began to carry their own burden for their inmate on drugs. They gained a new outlook on the behaviors and needs of those inmates.

The Master works in strange ways, and He can use you. It is all in being a willing vessel of God. All of these things that were happening were part of the commitment I made to the Lord the day He healed me and filled me, and I praise Him every day for it.

My inmate needed surgery, and that meant she would go to the county hospital. By now, my husband had gotten permission to visit with her, too. She enjoyed having the two of us stop by. It was more like friends talking together than meeting a social worker. We shared the news at home and about our teenagers, and how the Lord was moving in their lives. For the first time, she began to think about others. She said that when she was paroled, she would like to go with me and tell others how crime and prison, from the time you're ten until you're twenty-five, can mess up your life.

This was a major turning point in her thinking and she felt she could express her emotions with us. By this time, we had many visits with her, had taken her children places, and given messages to her mother.

There is a responsibility here. These inmates have been misled so many times before. You need to ask the Lord to lead you all the way. One wrong word can break the friendship. It probably looks like a losing ballgame, but if that's the way it is, don't worry, for you will get one hundred percent in the end when the Lord asks,

"When I was in prison, and ye came unto Me." (Matthew 26:36)

I can say, "Lord, I did my best. I took the message to this one. I planted the seed you gave me, and led them to the living waters." Praise God.

You have to ask yourself, "What about your call? Is your calling in the prisons of this world? Are you in your own prison?" Let the light shine, for only then will they see the light of your life, Jesus Christ.

When the time came for the packages to be wrapped, the boys, some of them with hands still shaking from the drugs, came to help with the project. We packed and wrapped sixty-one boxes for the inmates. It was a true blessing for the relationship between those dedicated to God and those wondering what kind of love is this? Through the vine, we learned that all of the boxes were received and the Bibles were now inside the prison. Who knows how many are affected...and how! Only the Lord knows for sure.

You probably are wondering how I could keep up the pace for such a long time, and it's true that there were times when I didn't feel like it. There were times when I was in the valley of depression and other times when I was just too tired; I didn't feel like taking my one free day, Saturday, to drive for over two hours just to talk to someone

I barely knew, just to get back and drive the long trip back. It's the love that Christ puts in your heart that drives you onward, toward the cross and real peace and rest.

My Lord promised,

"Come unto me and I will give you rest." (Matthew 11:13)

I am a woman just like any other; a mother, a wife, with faces to wash, laundry to be done, and meals to be cooked. Thanks to my older daughters, they made much of my work possible. If they had not been there to care for the younger children, I would have been much more confined. They did receive a blessing from this, too. It's good for your children to see you give of yourself, so they understand what God expects of them. There are times that we forget because we get so wrapped up in other things that we forget our first and most important mission; our spouse and family. The Lord reminds me; sometimes softly, then more sharply when necessary.

Chapter 13
Trials

Now, more than ever before, problems started to happen to my family. I was so happy working for the Lord that it didn't strike me that life could get so messed up in such a short period of time.

My second oldest child went to the dentist. Unfortunately, on the day of the appointment it had rained and then froze, so the car got stuck in the ice. The boy who drove her and her sister decided to push the car. At that precise moment, she fell under the car; the wheels rolling right over her legs.

They were all so frightened by what had just happened that they picked my daughter up and brought her home instead of taking her to the hospital. Obviously, with such a severe injury, we rushed her directly to the hospital.

The hospital treated her injuries and told her to see a doctor as soon as possible. The doctor said that she was going to need surgery as soon as possible or she might lose her leg. We arranged for her to enter the hospital; then I just prayed and prayed.

Next, I began to fast. Our Christian friends meant so much to my daughter and me. We witnessed together at the hospital. It was the first time in months that we had really been alone together. She spent a week in the hospital and six weeks on the living room floor; talking to everyone who came into the house. This ended up being a great witnessing time for both of us. Her leg healed, and just as I thought things were getting better, they started to get worse.

Adam, our three-year-old, started having behavior problems. The devil was working overtime on us. I must not have been as *prayed up* as I had thought. Adam was hyperactive and the medicine was not working for him. We knew that he needed special education, so we enrolled him in the developmental clinic.

Just as our life was getting back to normal, my eight-year-old daughter started having pain in her stomach and vomiting. Her white blood count was over a thousand, which is much higher than the normal range for anyone. After some tests, the doctor found swelling in her bowels. They called in a surgeon and kept her in the hospital. In all the confusion of the arrangements, I was caught up in the world and not in my faith. This can easily happen to a Christian who doesn't watch every minute for Satan's traps. The blood count rose to twelve hundred. The surgeon said, "We can only wait a little longer to redo the surgery."

The next blood count was fourteen hundred. Just then, I realized that I hadn't really prayed for Laurie. Had I forgotten the promises of the Master? I was to call upon His name and I hadn't done it. I got on the phone and called some prayer warriors of mine and we agreed. The prayer was on its way to heaven. Also the answer was on its way. One more test and I would know if the prayer had been answered.

They prepared Laurie for surgery while they took one last test. The surgeon came in, excitedly exclaiming, "The count is down to one thousand!" Praise the Lord!

I sat with Laurie, watching her sleep, asking myself how man can choose not to walk a constant walk with the Master, for He is truly the Master in everything that happens to you and me. I told the doctor, "You know who did that, don't you? It was the Man upstairs." He replied that he had seen a boy walk who hadn't been able to walk for over two years and he'd been healed through prayer. This was the first doctor I had met who had seen the touch of the Master.

We all forget what the Master is like. Just as the Bible teaches, He is like a good Father. He knows just what and how to teach us. There are many times that if it had not been for His guiding hand, it would have been sheer disaster. All I know is that I have everything to make me happy. I have Jesus. Do you know the Jesus I know? He can heal a sick soul, a torn leg, a blood condition. If you don't, friend, start searching today for Him.

Adam's problem grew worse and worse as the days went on. He bit everybody, kicked and screamed, and with everything else going on, it finally got to me.

I decided to go to a prayer meeting being held in Dayton, to get away and clear my thoughts. The night turned out to lead me into a realm, which at the time I could hardly believe. The burden of the past few months had been heavy, but I also had the same problem which a lot of you mothers do. My oldest daughter had not really realized what Jesus could mean in her life and this was the biggest burden on my heart.

Chapter 14
What Trial?

The church service began. We sang and praised the Lord just as we did every Sunday at church. The preacher asked all those who needed prayer to come forward. A friend next to me whispered, "Go forward and let him pray for you." I declared, "My Lord knows my needs." It wasn't that I wouldn't go forward, just that I was so exhausted.

Many church goers went forward and the preacher ministered to each of them. Then, without warning, he came to where I was sitting, reached out his hand, and took me forward. I'll never forget when he said, "The Lord loves you, but there is one more trial He has for you." I raised my hands to my face and began to cry. He went on, "For you will go to the pits of hell. You must lift up your hands and praise Me, for I will not forsake you." There was much more said that day, but these words are the part I remembered the most…for within three days, I was in the pits of hell.

Some things happen to us in order to test us to see if we can withstand the pressure. He is really preparing us for a greater walk with Him. I just praise His name. He knew I would not forsake Him. God also knew that a few souls were crying out for help, and He knew that I would bring the message to them; that the Master is with them throughout everything in life. Now, I feel that He allowed everything to happen, even though it was caused by the devil, for I learned many things in that hell.

On Saturday, just three days after the preacher told me of the hell I would be in, I started to cry. I don't know what happened. I lost control completely. I wanted to see a Christian doctor; someone who could understand my convictions. Unfortunately, most of them were out of town. The one doctor he did find ordered a room for me in a hospital in another town.

I don't remember much about the first day or so. One thing I do remember was the countless questions about religion, like "Do you believe in a man named Jesus?" I realized that I was in that pit of hell the preacher had told me about. The language in the hospital was enough to make you sick. The freedom to talk about Jesus was taken away, for I could talk to no one at this place. Where was I? Was this real or a nightmare? It was real, all right. It was beyond belief. People screaming, cursing, and lusting; surely this was the devil's playground, the very pits of hell.

When my husband came, I told him about their questions about religion. He could hardly believe what I was saying. He promised to call the doctor as soon as he got home.

Suddenly, a woman entered the room. She had gone out on a pass and came back intoxicated and unruly. The liquor, combined with her medications, caused her to get a little wild. The hospital staff just left her, huddled in a corner and crying. I felt I had to go and pray with her. I said to my husband, "Let's go over there and pray for her." He replied, "Just let her be, you don't know how mentally ill she is...and she might be dangerous." But when the Holy Spirit calls, you comply. He knew me well enough to know that no one could stop me; not to mention, I was already halfway over to her. I asked her if she wanted us to pray with her.

"Oh, please do," she begged us, and so we did. I told her, "If you believe that Christ is the answer, get in bed and go to sleep." She arose from the floor and got into bed. Praise the Lord.

By this time my husband had had enough. He said he had to get out of this place, that it would drive anyone crazy. He left, and what I thought was to be a quiet night turned into another nightmare. The nurse came in and started shaking her. I told her that she was sleeping, but the nurse just shook her even more.

"She has overdosed," the nurse said. "No," I told her, "she is just sleeping."

There was no use explaining what had taken place earlier that day. They wouldn't understand. About this time, three other men came in and everything in the room started to fly. The woman came out of the bed like the devil himself was after her. She began screaming and throwing everything she could get her hands on; including people. I crawled out of the room on my hands and knees. At this point, I remember another part of the prophecy the preacher had given to me; that when I get on my knees, raise my hands and praise Him, He will help me. There, in that violent confusion, I knelt and raised my hands to the Lord. He had healed me. If you ever get in a place like this, call upon the name of the Lord.

Chapter 15
Reality

The very next day, the hospital staff said that I had to do something to show that I was accepting reality. They wanted me to clean off the tables and empty the ash trays. When my husband heard of this news, he called the doctor and told him, "She came here for a rest, not to clean the hospital. If you want to start a Bible study, she will be more than glad to help, but she's not cleaning." I guess the doctor thought we were both a little crazy, but my husband's determination made it so. They moved me to another floor, where I was permitted to talk with other patients.

There were many I talked to; some with problems bigger than I had and some with less. I had life with Christ, so I knew there was a tomorrow, but many of them had nothing. As I started to witness, I guess the devil thought he had to get me out because I was given a four-hour pass. I picked up some Bibles and went back with victory in my heart.

The doctor said my religion put me in the hospital, but if it hadn't been for my religion, I would never have gotten out. I can't think of a better reason to go to a hospital than for my strong belief in Jesus Christ. I was privileged to carry such a great burden for my fellow man that it exhausted me.

I was told I would have to take some kind of occupational therapy as part of my treatment. While I was there, they let me make a belt for my husband that said "Jesus Is Love" on it. The worker said, "Your husband will never wear that." I replied, "You don't know my husband." Every time he wears it, I end up telling someone how I went into the pits of hell and came out on the mountain.

There are others who need God's help in these hospitals...these asylums. If you get nothing else out of reading about my experience, go to one and share with them the healing power of Christ. They need to know. They might be waiting there right now. There were some I met and prayed with and others I shared with.

You will never realize what getting into a place like that can do to an unsaved person or to a new Christian. You must go to them, for the hour is coming when there will be no more time to say you'll do it tomorrow. And again the question will be put to you,

"I was sick, and ye visited Me..." (Matthew 26:36)

All things will have to be answered; even those thoughts of the heart. The Bible tells us this.

"Watch therefore, for ye know neither the day nor the hour wherein the Son of man cometh." (Matthew 25:13)

When I returned home, things got back to normal; rolling along just as before.

A girl from a school for the blind was to be our next walk with the Master. She had called the church for someone to give her a ride. She was from St. Louis and didn't know anyone in Cincinnati. That evening there were two from the blind home, next there were three, and by the next Sunday there were four. We had to take a course at the Center to learn how to care for them. What does God have in store for us next?

Chapter 16
Life in a Spirit

You meet many people in life. Some are passing acquaintances, while some you remember often. One Sunday a special person came into my life. I wanted a special blessing and I asked the Lord to use me in a special way. This question you do not ask Him lightly, for He will give you what you ask for.

As the services ended, I felt compelled to go to the rear of the church and give someone my phone number. I asked my husband to stay behind with the blind people and told him that the Lord had spoken to my heart; I needed to give my number to someone.

In that moment, I had no idea who needed my number, but was led to a small, dark-haired girl. I say girl, because she looked young to me at the time. I introduced myself and told her I felt she should have my phone number. Nothing more was said at the time. I simply thought she was a visitor of the church who might be having marital problems or something else where I could help.

The next day the phone rang. I was quite surprised to hear from her so soon, but as the conversation went on, I found out that she was a new Christian and very much needed someone to talk to. I didn't get much done that day. We talked on the phone for three hours about her new-found Jesus. Previously, she had been a stripper in a nightclub, she had been using drugs for eight years, and if Christ hadn't come into her life, she's not sure where she would be. The two of us became close friends; phoning and seeing each other often.

My new friend lived in her own apartment, but she had to move in order to move forward in her Christian life. Everything seemed so hard for her.

We don't always recognize how very hard it can be for the new babe in Christ; those with backgrounds like hers. They have been used, beaten, and misled so many times, that they are surely lambs among wolves. Many a tear was shed for her sins which had to be overcome. Her life had to change so much. She had to change so much. She needed a fellow Christian to love her, guide her, and pray with her; regardless if it was midnight or three in the morning. To share one another's burdens is a great task, and must be handled with love and care.

"Bear ye one another's burdens, and so fulfill the law of Christ." (Galatians 6:2)

She had questions for me, like, "What will people think of me? Am I walking the way the Lord wants me to?" And the main one, "Am I good enough?"

Oh, the lonely heart of this girl when we met. She loved Christ, but did not stand on His promises. She claimed she couldn't make it. We called each other every day; talking until the wee hours about the love of Jesus Christ.

It was around this same time that a man, who had been in jail for murder for over eight years, was at the Challenge Center. He gave his life story about how Jesus had saved him from sure death.

I asked a friend of mine if he might ask this man to talk to my friend. They had both had the same kind of life and knew the talk of the street well enough to understand each other. When he called her, he asked if she would like to go to the church with him. She made it clear to him that she had no intention of going to church or anywhere else with him. Still, bright and early that next Sunday morning he was at her door. She relented, and so began another story for two lonely people. They each needed someone to talk to and wanted to work for the Lord. The connection worked so well that they ended up getting married.

This man had not known a Christmas on the outside for twelve years. This meant his social life was not developed either. He had lived hard, and so had she; he on the inside, she on the outside. She had men at her feet before; money at the wink of an eye, cars, and anything else she wanted. On the other hand, he had survived with nothing, fighting for everything he got, and getting it anyway he could find.

The first thing was to get him a job. This would not be easy unless, of course, you have the help of the Lord. He was interviewed for three different jobs and was hired at four dollars an hour. Since he was not going to make a lot of money at this new job, the worry of making the monthly bills was still a concern...so they moved in with us to save enough money to get them started.

It was a real crowd, my family, the two of them, her daughter, and their two dogs. It took some adjustment, but we all made it work. There were times when we goofed up and there were times when we had love all around us. The situation worked out with our family, but, unfortunately, the two of them still had troubles. They needed to get deeper into the Word of God and to ask the Lord for guidance. We would explain what the Word meant about things in particular; then we would say, "Don't blame us. Talk it over with the Lord."

Things worsened between the two of them and she decided to move out. There was no way for us to explain the seriousness of what she was doing or that going back on pills was not the answer.

Why put such a testimony in with all the miracles? Because it is the truth and these things happen. If our faith is not strong enough to stand up under such conditions, it is not real faith. At first, I felt that maybe we had failed; but then I realized that we had only planted the seed. He is the one who knows who shall come and take up the cross and follow Him. The strength which is given to us today is what we must go forward with, not what we feel we must do ourselves.

There are still moments when I remember standing on the terrace and burning pictures and g-strings as this girl sang to herself, "He Touched Me." The Lord has given us many privileges, and as time goes on, I think I see a little more of the true meaning of being a servant of the Lord. Not for me, Lord, but that Thy glory might reach someone, somewhere, tearing himself to pieces, and tell him that all he needs is Jesus.

Part Two
One Way Farm

Introduction - Part Two

In 1976, after much prayer, my husband, our children, and I decided to start a ministry. Working with people who are homeless or in need, those who come from within the walls of prison, and now we decided to work with teens, too.

We had been searching for over a year for a place to start such a ministry. Then, one Sunday at church, a gentleman approached me and said, "I understand that you are searching for a place to start a ministry. I have a piece of property that would work well for you. It's really not for sale, but when I got to heaven I don't know how I could explain it to the Lord if I didn't let you have it. So, go on and look at it and see what you think."

In order to be sure that we were doing what the Lord wanted us to, we created a fleece. A fleece is a reference to the story of Gideon in Judges 6. Gideon asked God for a sign to show he was doing what God wanted him to do. According to *our* fleece, our place had to have the following: It needed to be fifteen minutes from church, fifteen minutes from work, have a couple of barns, and a couple acres of land.

When you are a new Christian, you don't quite understand the hand of God. We should have asked for as much acreage as we could get, because later on we had to pay seventy-seven thousand for the acreage adjoining our two acres. But at the time, we didn't know what the Lord had in store for us.

We had a vision that we would like to have a couple of fireplaces, and that we probably will need to do some renovating; a new roof, a hot water heater, and other updates. We wanted everything redone in this particular house, but at a price we could afford. So, we ventured out to take a look at this piece of property.

The starting point was our church; then from there it took us only fifteen minutes to get to the farm. As we began to look around, we were amazed to find that the building already had two fireplaces, a new roof and hot water heater, it had been rehabbed throughout, and even a few barns that were going to need some help. All of this was situated on a couple of acres, making it a perfect location for our needs.

What did the house cost? Well, the price the gentleman wanted was way too high for us. We didn't have *that* kind of money. Even though we had recently sold a house of mine, another one that my husband had, and we were debt free, we only had a certain amount of money to start the ministry. We explained to the man that the price was too much for us to take on; giving him details about our fleece. Everything in the fleece had been realized except for the price.

The gentleman asked us to have the property appraised again, so we could determine the true worth of the property. Much to our liking, the price came in much lower than the asking price. Unfortunately, the gentleman said he would not sell it for that price. We began to feel ill about this particular dream coming to an end. We knew the Lord would guide us in the right direction, but where?

Then, after a brief hesitation, the gentleman said, "Have the property reappraised again. I will meet in the middle, between the low appraisal and the next appraisal." When the next appraisal came in, it was a price that we could afford, which meant all the requirements of the fleece had been met. Yeah for us!

After much forethought and reflection, we purchased the property and One Way Farm was ready to be born. Soon after, two semi-trucks, five children, and two adults embarked upon a lifelong commitment. One Way Farm was a reality and the Lord trusted us to begin a life of serenity, with times of troubles and miracles, with His hand in ours.

When I started writing this book, I could not believe how blessed I had been, how many things had happened to us and our lives, and how everything seemed to fit into where One Way Farm is today. I started to draw on a piece of construction paper the vision the Lord gave me and the road map to the final vision.

"Where there is no vision, the people perish." (Proverbs: 29-18)

The final vision is exactly where I want to be, but not necessarily where I saw myself ending. It's funny how life, with the Lord's touch, works out that way.

Chapter 17
The Way of Miracles

Now begins the story of how the One Way Farm was set in motion, how the vision began, and how the Lord held my hand throughout the entire process. The time is now thirty-one years later, year 2009, and in that time there have been a tremendous amount of events and miracles that have occurred. The Lord walked every step of the way with us.

First and foremost, we started working exclusively with children instead of adults.

One story, in particular, that I remember was when a State Inspector came to the home and started looking around; telling me that I didn't have enough air molecules for the number of people that I had living in the house. He told me that we would have to build an addition. Since we didn't really have the money to build on an addition, I sat and pondered and prayed on this issue. How are we were going to build with no money? But, as I have seen many times before, God always has a plan in order. Oh, so many plans.

A lady heard about our dilemma and called me. She said, "I have been watching your work. I will buy all the materials to build the addition." I was so excited of the news and praised God, "Thank you, God, for giving us the addition we needed!" Oh, I didn't know how important that prayer was at the time and how much it meant.

One thing I didn't think about at the time was who was going to build it? We didn't have the money to hire anyone. I did find out that if you are a private homeowner, you can build or remodel your home yourself. The problem was we didn't know how to work with electric, put up a building, or even what supplies to buy.

After everything was delivered, a gentleman stopped over to take a look at the load. He said, "Where are your trusses? You have to have trusses in order to build" "What are trusses?" I asked. (That is how much I knew about building, I felt so dumb and blessed at the same time!) He replied, "Those are the things that hold up the roof." He then added, "I will take care of the trusses for you."

This wonderful man called the company he worked with (he was a major builder) and told them that we needed trusses. Praise God, the trusses came. The trusses were installed by volunteers and we went on our merry way.

Still, there were so many things that had to be done. What should I do? Who can help us? First, we could not have a span of more than 40 feet. It was going to be a tight fit, but we would make it; 40 feet, one inch. We had to put in reinforcements, but first we had to tear part of the roof off of the old house. That is when the church group stepped forward to help. These kind souls tore off the old roof. Eventually, we had the new addition completed and under roof. God had all of these people to help us. Praise God!

Everywhere we looked there were blessings. Each time there was a problem to be solved, the Lord came to us. I had two boys living with me at the time, both who were taking drywall classes at a local vocational school. I also had an electrician and plumber on my Board of Directors. I remember when we tried to do the drywall; we would look at it, realizing that we didn't install it right. It would crack and we would end up having to redo the wall all over again. Piece by piece, the tile would stay in place. We bought everything we needed as we got each contribution. Eventually, piece by piece, each of us put our addition together. This gave us more than enough of the air molecules necessary to house the kids, and we were on our way. We got our finished addition.

Instead of the whole family sitting on the steps with only one bathroom, waiting to go in or take a shower, we had two additional bathrooms...praise God! It made life quite more comfortable. I remember when the addition was finished and all the children that were there, my husband, and I, all laid our hands in the cement. Kind of like a finished comment; that it was done and praised God. Little miracles began to become bigger ones. For some, the purpose in one's life, like "My Commission," they are much simpler.

My Commission

"To work each day with love and heart
This is my simple part
To see the eyes that cry, and tear, and stare
To know that God has chosen you to be there
To see the simple smile upon their face
To know that you have made a place
A place for them to learn and grow
This is my commission that I must sow."

Chapter 18
Manual Alarm

One of the first things we did when we moved in was put a sign up for One Way Farm. There was already an old sign out in front, being held up with railroad ties, so we decided to put our sign there. First, we had to get all the letters we needed for the name; then we painted and placed each one onto the board left for our new venture. This was the day One Way Farm was created.

Unfortunately, it wasn't too long after that when the Building Inspector arrived. He inquired, "Who gave you permission to put up that sign? This is a residential area and signs are not allowed." His explanation of the law certainly was scaring me!

As confidently as I could, I replied, "I didn't put it up, I just cleaned it up." We learned that it was an existing sign that had been there since 1927…which meant it could stay! The Lord knew we needed that sign, He knew we would never be able to get a new sign approved with the area being zoned residential so He had put the sign up in 1927, so that in 1976 we could clean it, repaint it, and Praise God! I live with new miracles happening every day; that is how the circumstances and situations transpire throughout this book. Just believe and step out in faith and into our service.

Oh, good…another issue. The Fire Inspector came to inspect the property and said, "You cannot have children living here; first, there are certain things that have to happen. You must install a manual fire alarm, all the doors have to open inward, and all the locks have to be a certain way." Well, even though the house was built in 1890, God knew then how to put the doors on. However, I was still without a manual fire alarm system.

When I checked how much manual fire alarm systems were, I knew we were in trouble. We did not have three or four hundred dollars just sitting around for a manual fire alarm! Now what do we do? Simple! I came to the conclusion that a manual fire alarm system was simply something you could just ding, and as long as it was loud enough to hear all over the house, it correlates with being a manual fire alarm. So I went to the hardware store, bought yard dinner bells for one dollar and forty-nine cents, and we were set.

I had those bells placed all around the house. Of course, all of the children were tempted to ding them on occasion, so I don't know how well they would have worked in a real emergency, but we were able to pass inspection in the meantime. Tribulations like the manual fire alarm seemed to happen all the time as we settled in, but there was always an answer or someone who could help.

Chapter 19
The Floors Began to Shake

After a year of getting through most of the trials placed upon us, we started our Friday Night Coffee Houses. A Coffee House is when Christians gather to praise the Lord. The children and young adults loved the drive out to our home, which at that time seemed like being in the country, and they loved being able to be in a Coffee House. We provided all sorts of refreshments, music, and everything else necessary to have a Coffee House for the youngsters. Sadly, this was at a cost that we didn't realize at the time.

We had so many people coming into our home at the time that we actually had to run speakers from the living room, through the parlor, the dining room, and into the kitchen. Due to so many people being in our house at one time, we noticed the floor was beginning to buckle from the extra weight. We knew that we were in for more expenses than we had bargained for in our plan.

We found our first issue began when we couldn't find any other type of brace that would work due to the height of the old basement walls, but as usual God already had a plan for us. We had a barn on the property that was being torn down at the time, and since it had long, sturdy beams that were equal to the length we needed in the basement of our house, we had our answer.

Once we had all our plans in place, the people from our prayer meeting put the beams in to brace the floor overhead. We braced up our house because praising the Lord was about to tear down our floor; especially when people got excited and began to clap and jump. There again, this was just another step that we went through to praise the Lord. Luckily, with support from others and prayer, we were able to continue the prayer meetings; not to mention, our groups kept growing, growing, and growing.

Just as we started to get a little comfortable, all of a sudden, we heard the sound of a threatening crack. A very large elm tree just fell onto our garage, smashing everything in its path. Well, you just look at it and say, "Oh God, my garage has been smashed to pieces. What am I going to do?" In our case, it was a blessing from God.

I had already been talking to people, saying, "If only we could build a bigger building there; then, we would have a bigger place to have our prayer meetings." Amongst all my chatter, a kind gentleman stepped up and offered to build a new building for us. He built a beautiful 20x40 building and all the people who attended the Coffee Houses and prayer meetings pitched in. Soon, this building became the location for our Friday night prayer meetings. What we didn't know at the time was that this was only the first of many buildings that One Way Farm would build.

The economy was really tough on everyone, but still people would leave money everywhere. I don't know how we did it, but we would just believe by faith that we could make this work. What was so extraordinary is that when we did have our meetings, people would fill up the building…even overflow it at times. When it was necessary, we would open up all of the windows and people would lean in just to be part of the group session. It reminded me of when Paul spoke in the caves and people would crowd around the holes in the caves to listen. It was truly a moving experience.

One Friday, a gentleman handed me a painting. It was a painting of Christ holding our little garage, with tears falling from his eyes. When I asked the man what the picture meant, he replied "When Christ sees how much faith there is in the little garage that he holds in his hands, he can't help but cry." We named that building, "The Little Mustard Seed," but later we changed the name to "The Mighty Oak."

Chapter 20
First Date

I always felt a bit guilty because I was either going somewhere, doing something, or figuring out what I needed to do next. I felt guilty about not being with my children at a certain time or doing special things with them. Like the time my daughter had her first date and I happened to be in Louisville at the time. I called her later that night to ask how her date went. She plainly said, "Great!" I could hear the disappointment in her voice; me missing her first date, not being there to make sure she was dressed all right, not taking her to the door, was a really sensitive point for her. I knew I couldn't change what transpired, but I could try to make it up to her in some small way.

Later, I saw the Norman Rockwell print, *First Date*, in a store that I just happened to walk into. I bought the print, had it framed, and wrote her a little note on the back. I wanted so badly to bring her some comfort.

The picture must have touched her in some way because later, when I went to see the house she had just moved into in Raleigh, NC, there were only two things on the wall. One was a puzzle I had put together and framed and the other, in a very prominent place, was the picture *First Date*.

Creating memories for children that can never be washed or taken away is actually the inner spirit that you have to give. When we make things for people, or when we have things we want to do, we may think, "Oh, it should not be like that," but it has its own signature and you should be proud of your work. It is a gift of love.

Chapter 21
Just Resting

There are many things that happen to you in life that make you think, "Oh, I just don't know what to do." I remember the days when we didn't have a van; therefore, we didn't have proper transportation for the children. We prayed and prayed for a vehicle that would allow us to bring others in need to us. Since then, I have learned how to designate my prayers. After you read this book, you will see a lot of places where I should not have put restrictions on my prayers. God does not see restrictions in us or what we need.

Just as with many of my prayers, this one was finally answered. Someone donated a van to us. It was red with a round porthole in the back panel. The entire inside of the van was carpeted; sort of like a hippy van. All I know is that the vehicle ran and that was all that we were interested in.

One day I was extremely tired, but we had plans that day to take all of the children to the movies. Altogether, there were fifteen of us. I became so weary that I finally had to get away, so I decided to go elsewhere on my own.

I took an extension cord, a heater, my inspirational tapes, and I took off to Hueston Woods, a campground near our home. There I was, sitting in the van at Hueston Woods, resting peacefully, when all of a sudden there were several loud knocks on the door. Startled by the intrusion, I looked out, and standing there were two police officers. All at once, I realized that from the looks of my van, they must have thought something else, like drugs or sex, must be going on inside. I assured them that nothing was going on; explaining who I was and why I was there.

I told the police officers that the van was the only transportation we had, and since our home was open to children in need, there was no place else for me to go to be alone. I told them that I had no money for a hotel, so I came to Hueston Woods to sleep in the van. Finally, I convinced them that I was just a lady sleeping in a van.

After the police left, I laid back down. I was uncomfortable so the rest I was trying to attain was not working out that well. All of a sudden I heard another noise. This time, however, it wasn't from someone knocking on the door.

The sound was coming from on top of the roof. Cautiously, I opened the door and looked up. There, sitting on my roof, was a huge vulture, scratching itself and luring at me.

Now, I decided it was time to leave and go home. I started to wonder about the children, too. I cared a great deal about all of them, but I was truly tired. I knew I needed them as much as they needed me.

As I drove home, the vulture followed me for some way. I could never figure out why, but later, I wrote this poem.

Can you give it all up?

"The boy came, his age sixteen
He started off being really mean
His temper was that "I'll get you today"
This boy meant, "I don't care what you say"
I heard a crash in the dining room
There he sat in this gloom
A gift I had had for some years
I then could feel my tears
All of a sudden a voice within
That I had heard now and then
"Can you give it all up
If you go my way?"
I could hear the voice say"

"Her eyes were blue and her hair dark

She always had a nasty remark
She took others' things with no care
Then, when asked, she would just stare
Then one day my wedding ring was gone
Then, when I asked her, she said
"Hey, you're putting me on."
Then she explained she gave it to a friend
I knew then I would never see it again
All of a sudden a voice within
That I had heard now and then
"Can you give it all up and go my way?"
I could hear the Master say."

"I have learned in the past
The things so cherished
And dear won't last
The thing that is a treasure to me
Is what faith has done, as you can see."

Chapter 22
Manna

You know that you are always supposed to pray for manna. Manna is help from heaven in the form of food, water, and the necessities of life. We were in desperate need of food and other essential items because on Friday there would be close to twenty-five young people who would spend the night at our house. On Saturday morning, I would get up and cook bacon, eggs, biscuits, and gravy. The children would sit around, read their Bibles, and praise God. We would have music, which included some of the children who played guitars. The event was always a very peaceful time.

One Saturday morning my husband came in and said, "Did you pray for bacon?" I replied, "Yes, I did. We need bacon badly." He responded, "Well, it's not quite ready yet." He ushered me out the front door to show me what he was talking about. To my amazement, sitting right outside our door were two little pigs. I guess it was manna falling from heaven.

I tried to keep the pigs; however, keeping pigs is another story for someone who is totally inexperienced in the care and feeding of such animals. Soon after our find, I learned of a man who raises pigs. He had lost most of his herd when they were struck by lightning during a bad storm. He still had a few pigs left, but his herd was much smaller than it used to be. With this new information, I decided to call him to see if he would be interested in taking these little pigs off my hands. He replied, "Yes, absolutely!" and with that he was on his way.

When the gentleman arrived, he was confused by these particular pigs. He said, "I'll definitely take them, but these pigs are from New Hampshire. What are they doing here?"

The second element of this wonder is that we began to talk and became fast friends. He appreciated the work we were doing for the children and the community and wanted to help in some way. He supplied us with drinks for the children and every year he would visit to find out what we needed. When I think about him and those pigs, especially since these pigs were not from around here, it is another clear example of a miracle walking into our lives.

At that same time, my freezer decided to go out. I had another farmer who had just slaughtered a pig for us so we would have bacon and other meats for the children. Now, without a working freezer, all of this food would go bad.

Just as I was getting ready to tend to the broken appliance, I saw a young girl, who had been the victim of a violent crime, sitting in the corner and crying. Of course, I had to help her so the freezer had to wait.

I sat down in the rocking chair and consoled her as best I could. After much time, prayer, and conversation, she seemed to settle down a bit. She was upset and in tears because of what she had gone through and by now I was crying because I had lost all of our food. I continued to rock her, sobbing and prayer, when there was a knock on the door.

Without any interruption to my task at hand, I told the visitor to come in. As the door opened, there were four of them. They just heard that we lost all of our meat and had come to clean out the freezer and refill it with new items. The Lord knows your needs and by faith they are fulfilled. These kind souls, who came in while I was rocking this girl, are still contributors today.

You see, there was nothing that ever happened to us without something far greater happening; something that created a solution to our problem. For when you walk in the light, the Master holds your hand.

Times were so tough that one of my daughters lived out of donation bags, too, because we could not afford new clothes. At Christmas time we had a lot of friends who would buy her gifts. With each gift, she would get very excited. Her favorites were a gold cross and a makeup case.

One day, this thirteen-year-old girl went to school as she did every school day. The difference was that on this particular day there was another girl leaving One Way Farm. She left, but then told her caseworker that she had forgotten something back in the room. This was the same room where all of the children kept their belongings. This young girl went back to the room and took all of my daughter's clothes and jewelry; including the gold cross. When she got home from school she learned that everything of hers was gone. Being a young teenager, she was extremely upset because she had lost a lot of her favorite mementos. With so little to begin with, and being so grateful for what she did have, this betrayal was more than she could handle.

Our cluster of friends heard of this unfaithfulness and knew that they had to do something for my daughter. Soon after the incident, these amazing friends came to our home and gave her five hundred dollars so she could buy replacement clothes. They even told her that if she needed more money, they would give it to her.

When the theft occurred, I had told my daughter that God never removes anything without giving something far greater in return. Since most of her clothes had either come out of garbage bags or she had made them herself, this new gift was even greater than what she had before. The woman who had bought her the cross purchased another cross for her. Each of our friends who had brought her a memento went out and bought a new memento for her.

With the generous gift of money in hand, my little girl and I went to the mall to restock her closet. What happened next was the biggest gift of all. She had all of this money, but just stood there and cried, "I just want to go home, take me home." She was so overwhelmed by the whole situation, and how God worked His magic, that she could not bring herself to spend the money.

Eventually, with enough time and guidance from me, she did go shopping, but it was a powerful lesson to teach a thirteen-year-old girl what was most important...God. He will never take anything away without giving you something far greater in its place.

Chapter 23
Mom, I Can Do This

I know I have talked quite a bit about my thirteen-year-old daughter throughout the book, and if you don't mind, I would like to tell you about something else that happened to her. Believe me, sometimes you may have it on your heart that you want to do this or that, but when it comes to thinking that your children are going to get hurt in some way, that overpowers your desire to do anything else.

My daughter went to bed earlier than usual for a school night because she was going to try out for cheerleading the next day. Then, one of the girls came into her room, making all kinds of noise. My daughter told her to go to sleep, which made this girl very mad. Mad enough that she started hitting her with an iron. I was so upset that I said, "This is it, we are not going to do this anymore. When you start getting hurt, that is the end of sharing our home with other children."

My daughter's reply stopped me in my tracks. She replied, "Mom, I can take the iron, I can take the hits. If we don't help these kids, no one else will."

I understood what she meant…and agreed with her. When I saw how much my daughter had learned, especially during what had just happened, I thought, you know there were stripes that He took and thorns on His head. If a thirteen-year-old girl is willing to take this kind of abuse, and understands that these children have to be taken care of, that is a miracle in its own right.

My daughter, now living in North Carolina, raised two sons, and then decided to go back to college. She enrolled into college, worked toward a degree in child development, and in June 2009, graduated with honors. I am so proud of her.

Chapter 24
The Donation Box

This story takes place in 1978, when the blizzard hit in December of that year. Each year our beautiful Nativity scene was set up outside and it would draw tremendous crowds. That particular Christmas, as we put the finishing touches on our work, it began to snow…and snow, and snow, and snow. It snowed so much that on Christmas Eve it was a white out. My husband said, "We might as well not open this event today because no-one is going to show up." I replied, "We put this event out there especially for Christmas Eve, and I believe someone should be out there, regardless if anyone shows up."

As usual, our house was filled with people everywhere, so I was glad to go out. I thought that being in a quiet place would be a good time for me to sit and reflect.

The forecasters were reporting that the storm was at a level three, which meant that no one was allowed on the roads, but I still went outside. The evening was bitter cold and I remember taking the straw from the bails to cover my legs and feet. I just sat there, the heat lamps helping with the wintry weather a little, but it was still freezing.

Through the quiet coldness, I thought I saw something moving around. We had a donation box, but it was in the front. I brushed it off, deciding that it must be the wind.

After a long while, I realized no one was going to come, it was getting late, and I was getting colder by the minute. With the swaddled doll baby in one arm, I picked up the donation box, and set off toward the house.

When I entered the house, everyone was joking, asking me how many donations I got…believing that certainly no one would have come out in this weather. Being the caretaker of the Nativity, I knew no one had come; however, much to our amazement, when I opened the box, there was a check and a note inside. The note simply said, "I was on my way to see my son, when I saw the manger. And in that manger was a woman holding a Christ-like child. This is my tithe for the year; I am the Ambassador to Belgium." There was a check for fifteen hundred dollars.

You may be wondering how the Ambassador to Belgium ended up near One Way Farm that evening. Well, his son lived in Fairfield and he was heading toward his house. Imagine that!

Does this story make you think about the Wise Men who came to visit the manger? Just imagine…the Ambassador to Belgium, fifteen hundred dollars, and more than what we made the entire season! This was one Christmas miracle and the star in the night that leads us.

Chapter 25
Christmas at One Way Farm

Since Christmas comes every year, there is always room for many Christmas stories. This is another Christmas story I would like to share before moving on.

We worked diligently on this Nativity; the old drummer boy, the Wise Men, and costumes made from old theater curtains. There were even doves flying. We spent so much time on every detail of our Nativity scene. Thousands came to see our display.

One night that year I sat and just watched the crowd. A little boy started to climb up onto the rail; halfway through, he said, "Come on Mommy, let's go. Let's go see Santa Claus."

She took the little boy's hand and started to leave. When she did, my spirit said, "No, she can't leave!" It was then that I added a new figure to our scene. I added Santa Claus.

Hastily, the narrator said, "Wait! There is still another guest to come. Santa knows most of all that the greatest gift to mankind was the Son of God."

Before long, I had church people calling me. They said that they would not come if I had Santa in the Nativity. I replied, "Please come by and see what Santa Claus is, before you decide."

The pastors had to come to the Nativity before they could advise their congregations to go. They just stood and watched. Then came the shepherds, the drummer boy, and there were animals all around. The script and monitor read, "There is still one more person who wants to come and honor the Christ child."

As everyone started to leave, they stopped as the Christmas character arrived. Santa simply walked up to the Nativity, knelt down on his knees in front of the manger, and handed a teddy bear to the Christ child.

The pastors returned to their churches and encouraged each of their congregations to go see the Nativity. All people have the right and grace to praise God.

Christmas on the Corner of One Way Farm

"Look! A manger and lights on the corner I see,
You know of whose honor it will be.
Everyone is laughing; father, mother, daughter, and son.
For what reason have they come?
There is a sign, what does it say?
'Road to Bethlehem–this way.'
Things seem much quieter than before.
Let's go closer, I want to see more."

"Lights twinkle and the crowd grows.
This is the miracle they spoke of, you know.
First come the little ones who climb the rail to peek.
Then come their parents to see whom they seek."

"Alongside auntie, comes grandmother, too.
Then, here comes the rest of the family crew.
Wait! There comes a thin man in tattered clothes.
As he walks in, he stands aside so no one knows.
In the glow of a dim candle light,
I can see a tear fall into sight."

"I walk over to greet the tall, thin man,
And reach out and hold his shivering hand.
As I look at this aged and worn face,
I know he has come at last, to the final place.
For where else would a broken man be,

Except at a manger where he can see
The one thing that lets him know
His life is worth living and encourages him to grow?"

"The night is heavy now and the night is cold.
They still come, the young and the old.
Can you imagine why on such a night,
That so many people would come to see such a sight?
I believe I know the answer to that.
It came when I saw a wheelchair, where a small boy sat.
His eyes lit up and a smile came to his face
And he bowed his head and a tear came into place.
There's hope in seeing the Savior born.
It's like the sound of a heavenly horn."

"There is hope and peace and love within.
Now is the time for your life to begin."

Chapter 26
Candy Love for Children

This next story is all too familiar to me. It has such a spiritual prompting, much like the St. Bernard someone brought to us. Her name was Brandy, and although that is a beautiful name, we felt it didn't fit her; so we named her Candy.

Candy was a loveable dog. She was a huge, typical St. Bernard who loved to run around and play with children. The kids got the love they needed and Candy loved them right back. She loved the children so much that I caught her in bed with them a couple of times. I would say, "Get out of that bed, girl. Get out, I said!" She would jump down and run to her resting place, until she found another opportunity to see the children. Eventually, she got so smart that she learned to wait until I went to bed, then she would go get back in bed with them. She was so big; it was like having a dog and a kid all rolled into one.

As the update to our facilities continued to progress, we knew the best place for Candy would be at the new Summerville Boy's Home location. She would have more freedom there and she especially loved being with the boys. It was a perfect fit for all. Everyone was so excited that the new location was finally ready.

When the building was completed, the boys moved in to the Summerville facility and Candy moved in right along with them. This faithful companion walked to the school bus every day with the boys, and she was there waiting for them every single day when they got home. Unfortunately, there was one thing she had to do in order to meet the boys when they came home from school; she had to cross the railroad tracks.

Regrettably, one day, Candy saw the boys coming, but she did not see the train, and that was the day she needlessly ran in front of the train and lost her life.

That big dog was never forgotten. The children never forgot about Candy because they realized how much she loved them. So much so that it was more important to run to them than anything else.

Through the Eyes of a Dog

Dedicated to Candy; a tan and white St. Bernard
who had over three hundred masters and friends at One Way Farm.

"I remember when I came;
They decided to change my name.
They changed my name from Brandy
To one much better called 'Candy.'
I was amazed to see so many faces,
Children coming from all kinds of places.
Into the boys' room I would sneak,
Because that is where I wanted to sleep
Nestled next to my newest friend,
And if possible under his hand.
I would run and chase them all,
And together we would fall.
I saw a man in a big white car;
I said to myself, 'I wonder who they are.'
A knock at the door and he walked in,
A boy with a small bag, I knew then.
I see them big and small and I love them all.
For a St. Bernard like me, this is my job as you can see.
As I watch them laugh and cry, I often sit and wonder why.
I was a gentle creature, but oh so great,

I guess that's why I was called a 'Saint'."

Candy was killed in the line of duty, waiting for her masters to come home. The children stopped because they saw a train, Candy did not. As she did many days before, she ran to meet the children, running in front of the train.

Candy.... an 8-year-old dog who was full of love.
Thank you for sharing your gift with One Way Farm
March 6, 1984

Chapter 27
The Story of a Widow's Faith and Fifteen Dollars

As our miracles continued on, there is one woman I will never forget. This story is about a widow's life and her faith beyond what you can imagine. Remember, all we have to do is believe; we must have the faith of a mustard seed.

We were on a very, very tight budget and we needed money so badly that I would find twenty dollars or more under a dish or some other hiding place from a visitor who knew our circumstances. My children were having a really hard time, too. I had all of them in a Christian school and it took everything we had to keep that going.

Today, we have a small building in the middle of our yard and I am going to tell how that building got there.

Before this tiny building, we were on such a tight budget that my husband had to put cardboard in the bottom of his boots because they had so many holes. Day after day, he would cut new cardboard inserts and put them in his boots.

During this time of hardship, budgeting for our food and bills, a woman came to us and asked, "My children are sick; do you think you could help me?" At the time, we only had fifteen dollars, which would buy lunches for the week and anything else that we needed. I asked her how much she needed and she said, "The prescriptions are fifteen dollars."

It was in that moment that the Holy Spirit moved upon me. I knew I had to give this woman the fifteen dollars. I handed her all the money we had and she left. In my faith, I understood that sometimes we don't understand the law of propriety until something like this happens. It is all a walk of faith.

To continue with the story, on our property, we had a small building where we had our prayer meetings and Coffee Houses. This was the building we had to rebuild after the tree fell on it.

Amongst our visitors, there was one elderly woman who would come to our prayer meetings all of the time. However, sometimes she would just come during the Coffee House and sit in the back, tapping her foot to the music. She was less than five feet tall, had a patch over one eye, dressed in older women clothing, and she always wore a colorful apron. Her hair was salt and pepper and nicely pulled back to show her face. She had one eye that was partially shut and she wore glasses. She always laughed with other visitors and she praised God. Since she was more than partially blind, someone would always have to bring her to the prayer meetings. Since she only lived about a mile away, sometimes we would take her food or medication when she needed it.

One day she called and asked if I could take her to the bank. I replied, "Well, yes, I can take you to the bank." So I went and picked her up and took her to the bank. As I sat in the car waiting, I started to wonder what was taking her so long.

Soon after, the petite, elderly woman came out of the bank with a bag in her hand. She handed me the bag and said, "My husband and I agreed that you were to have this. He passed away this morning. We want you to have this." When I got back home, I opened the bag; it had nine thousand dollars in it.

As excited as I was to see that kind of money offered for our mission, I felt I needed to give it back to the woman. I thought surely she needed that money as much, if not more, than we did. So I picked up the phone and told her that we couldn't accept her gift, but that we appreciated her thoughtfulness. She replied, "If you do not take the money, I will drop it in the box for the poor."

Eventually, I agreed to take the money she was offering...on one condition; that I spend it on people who I know have been through real difficulty and need some help. Of course, since we had a Coffee House and prayer meetings, I knew quite a few people who needed help; they needed their electricity turned on, tires for their car, clothes for their children, and so on.

I began to record the needs of those who visited, and then I went out to find more people who were in desperate need of some help. Finally, I spent all of the money this dear woman gave to us and I had it all recorded so I could show what I did with her gift. I was able to show where I bought tires for someone who needed to go see their daughter that they had not seen, I shared where I paid for electricity, bought clothes, medicine, and even where I bought a pair of boots. I had it all recorded, and I gave it to her.

Much to my surprise, she said, "The Lord still wants to give you something. You took all of this money that I gave you and you gave it all away. Because you gave it all away, he still wants you to have something for yourself. Make a list of the top ten things that you need; very expensive things that you need but can't buy and give me the list."

Things that I needed...where should I begin? I had a lot of dental work that needed to be done. We needed a fence for our horses, we needed our house insulated, and we needed tires. All of these items were expenses that we couldn't afford and I couldn't foresee where we were going to get the money. After much thought about all of our priorities, I gave her my list. All she said was "Come back tomorrow."

So, with a little confusion and a lot of curiosity, I went back the next day. As we sat down, she said, "You know, because you gave all of the money away that I gave you, the Lord wants you to have your heart's desire, so I calculated how much it would cost for all ten items, and here is the money." It was fifteen thousand dollars. Praise the Lord!

You really have to stop and think when things begin to move in this way...and if you don't, you ought to. If you stay in faith, you can really feel the Holy Spirit, not only guiding you, but also guarding you and providing for you.

At the time, I never really thought twice about taking care of people and what they need. It never entered my mind that she might do something more than purchase one item on my list. In the end, she bought the very first computer we ever had to run the One Way Farm Children's Home. You really have to stop and think when considering what someone might do to help those in need. Miracles are so misplaced by so many people and it is evident that they, miracles, are there. I see this miracle as how someone can take a mere fifteen dollars and turn it into nine thousand and then into fifteen thousand dollars.

I think about this story because of her generosity and because it happened so early in the stages of One Way Farm. In fact, it was around 1978 when all of this took place. What I have learned since then is to never underestimate the ability, or generosity, of another person. They might surprise you.

After everything settled down at her home and her husband was buried, I took notice that her house was in major disarray. I wanted to help her in some way, so I offered to clean her house. There was so much clutter that there was a path where you could walk from room to room.

What is odd about this whole situation is that I didn't really know this lady as well as I thought I did. Her house was in disarray, she wore worn and tattered clothes, yet oblivious to me, she had the means to have better. I took her food all the time, yet I never realized that she had money to help herself. I just thought she needed to be taken care of.

So off I went to clean her house. I noticed she had almost every Look Magazine for the past sixty years, and in the midst of all those magazines, I began to find U.S. War Bonds. By the time I finished cleaning her house, I had found twenty-eight thousand dollars worth of U.S. War Bonds. Isn't it amazing how God multiplied her money? When I mull this over, it is today's miracle, and since I must have one every day, this is *this* moment's miracle. Albeit, an absolute fabulous one.

It is awe inspiring for people to go on, when they hear of miracles happening to someone else. Many believers, whether constant in the word of God or not, need to hear of miracles. As for me, I live the miracles each and every day. I see the miracles in every aspect of my life.

I Won the Race

"One day long ago, I asked the Lord,
'Where will I go…?
What will be my part?'"

"He answered in that gentle voice,
'You have to have great faith
Right from the start.'"

"'There will be many trials to endure at first,
Keep the desire of faith and love of which you thirst.'"

"'Many times you will want to give up and quit the race,
But always know God has, for you, a special place.'"

"I can see the chapel, in my mind's eye, as I was shown…
I can hear the praises of children in a heavenly tone."

"No one will ever know the miracles that have taken place…
So I can finally say, 'I have won the race.'"

~ Barbara J. Condo

Chapter 28
Bright Light

I still remember in our early days at One Way Farm, money was really tight, but instead of worrying about thousands of dollars, as I do now, I just worried about dollars.

One time, I was in the kitchen counting what was left of the funds for the week. I only had thirty-nine dollars and I wondered how we would ever make it until the next check.

It was fall, and the leaves were falling quite heavily all around the porch. To get my mind off our money concerns, I decided to go out and sweep the leaves off the porch. When I did, I evidently became unconscious and fell. Startled by the noise, my daughter came out to check on me. She rushed over to me and began beating on my chest, while another friend called for an ambulance. After the life squad worked on me a bit, I was off to the hospital with family in tow.

Over the next several hours, I remember most of what was happening to me. I remember holding my hands close to my body, while I was moving upward, like being in a tunnel heading toward a light, and I was moving at an extremely, fast pace.

Suddenly, I began to smell honeysuckle, which was my father's favorite flower. I began to smell lilac, which were my aunt's favorite flowers and the lilac scent of the perfume she wore. It was then that I realized that I was in the midst of their souls.

Next, I began to hear two people speaking; one of them was angry, but I could not understand what was being said. The voice was aggressive and angry, and I finally could hear his words. All he would say was "Yes, I can!" The other voice sounded like it was in a white cloud. He would gently say, "No, you can't." Then the other voice would again respond very aggressively, "Yes, I can!" Finally the voice in the white cloud replied, "You can do anything you want to her, but you cannot take her life, only I can take her life."

At this point, I began moving at a very fast speed, back down the tunnel where I started. I remember waking up and seeing little clouds that said "Jesus first! Jesus first!" As I regained consciousness, I realized I was in the Mercy Hospital Emergency Room. The nurses knew who I was and they were gathered around me rebuking death.

Since that time, there have been a few things that have happened in my life. The power of that conversation between those two voices became evident to me throughout times of concern.

For instance, one occasion was when I had a car wreck. My van rolled over on the road three times before coming to a dead stop. By some miracle, I was laying on the side of the road, away from traffic, when the paramedics showed up. In that same moment there was a discussion going on in my head. One voice saying "Yes, I can!" and the other saying "No, you can't." "Yes, I can!" "No, you can't. Only I can take her life."

The next time this happened was later on in our ministry. I had to have a stent put in, but they accidentally cut an artery in the process. I lost a tremendous amount of blood, and in the midst of that crisis the voices came together again. One voice insisting that now was the time to take my life, and the other voice saying, "No, only I can take her home."

These moments, when voices are around me, have been *never forget* experiences. After each incident, when I think about the voices, and how I tried to hold my arms in tight so that I didn't hit the sides of the tunnel, the experiences have never left my mind. I know that I am blessed. I will always remember how mean and angry the one voice sounded, and, of course, we know who the other soft and gentle voice belonged to; the One who says, "No, you can't. Only I can take her life."

Chapter 29
An Unusual Answer to Prayer

You know, there are always so many things that we need. The list goes on and on, changing as we go. We constantly prayed for this and prayed for that, and graciously received the blessing for all that was given to us.

There is one miracle, however, I will never forget and I share the story repeatedly throughout my lifetime. One day, my administrative assistant came to me and said, "Barbara, we need to have a van. Our ratio on transportation is completely scheduled out. We must have a van in order to help anyone new in need."

One Way Farm could not purchase anything that substantial, and I was not able to dip into our personal finances either because I had cosigned for everything One Way Farm had bought. I was so tapped out financially that when I tried to buy a refrigerator for myself, I couldn't, so I knew I couldn't purchase a van.

I was so concerned about the whole situation that when I went to bed that night, I had a dream. In case you didn't know, it is stated in the Bible,

"…the old dream dreams." (Act 2:17)

I dreamt that I was to go to a local ticket office, (you know, a local place where people purchased tear-off tickets to win money), I was to take name tags with me, and I was to tell them that God had sent me there. I should tell them that they were to buy us a van.

That next evening, I had a Board Meeting. At the meeting a board member came to me and said, "Here are the name tags left over from the last fundraiser." I stopped dead in my tracks. Did she really just say that? This new information prompted me to tell the entire Board about my dream. Unfortunately, this sent everyone laughing, telling me that I was getting way too wrapped up in my dreams; especially that particular piece of scripture. Sure, I was more than a little hurt that the Board could not perceive that God would talk to me, but I knew better.

The next morning I woke up with that same dream...still very strong in my conscience, my subconscious, and in my spirit...so I took my son, along with the name tags that God instructed me to bring, and went up to the local ticket place.

When I got there, I told the owner of the ticket store about my dream and that God had sent me there. I also handed him the name tags that I was told to take to him in my dream. He asked me how much we needed to purchase the van. I answered, "It is twenty-seven thousand dollars." His reply was simply "Okay" and I was on my way with check in hand.

Here again, you cannot underestimate God, or determine or guess what God has in store for you. Is it for faith that you are willing to do the obnoxious, in order to confirm you heard the voice? Are you willing, when you see someone in a restaurant just ordering coffee but realizing that they want food, to take your money, walk up with no embarrassment, and lay ten dollars on the table?

I have seen people in restaurants, who have two or more children, ordering something for them to eat, and then cutting it up and dividing it up between themselves. I know they cannot afford anything more to eat and probably have to struggle in other areas, too. I'll go up to the cash register, pay their bill, and make comment that this is how we plant seeds. These are the same seeds that have developed One Way Farm into what it is today, and why it continues to grow.

When you see someone fall down, you pick them up. When you see someone hungry, you feed them. Whatever you can do will help. You have no need to tell anyone what you are doing, because the peace should come right inside of you, for it is that grace and spirit that brings pleasure.

Chapter 30
Before I Die

When we bought the house, we did not have any debt, we had paid it all off. Now, we were deep in debt and it was beginning to become a tremendous burden. My children did not have the clothes that they needed, my husband put cardboard in his shoes everyday because of the holes, but still we went on. We truly believed that this was where God wanted us. We settled into our farm, attempting to do anything and everything, and taking care of anyone who came to us.

One evening I had fallen asleep in the recliner and received a call around midnight, the stranger on the other end of the phone said, "I have a dime bag in my pocket, I am going to kill myself, and I just wanted to tell someone that I am going to do it. When I reached into my pocket, I found your card, so I called you."

I talked with this young man for quite some time, asking about his family and anything else that was troubling him. Then, I began to talk about the Lord, about death, and about how he could still make a contribution to life. We talked for what seemed over an hour; then suddenly he said, "Wait a minute, lady." and he left the phone. I was frantic. I did not know if he left the phone to kill himself or what, but I continued to stay on the line. After a while, he came back on the line and said, "I just wanted you to know something, lady. I flushed that dime bag down the toilet." I replied, "Praise God!" and we ended our conversation by saying "Good Night."

After the call, I fell back asleep. Then, all of a sudden, I had a deep sense that someone was standing over me. When I looked up, standing there over me was a burly, 6'4" man in ragged clothes. He had a frightening look on his face, mangled hands, and long, straggly hair. Gently, he whispered, "Lady, I am the man you talked to on the phone. I only wanted to come here and personally thank you for saving my life. Can I shake your hand?"

Obviously, I was taken back by the anxious awakening, but to reinforce that I trusted him in a Christian love, I replied "No, but you can hug me." He bent down to hug me and began to cry. Then, just as abruptly as he approached me, he left.

Strangers in the night, seeking only the love of a Christian to save their life, are begging for someone to care.

Chapter 31
The Promised Land

We are now at the stage where true miracles begin to happen at One Way Farm…as if there have not already been so much given to our mission. The key is that you have to watch for them every single day. The Bible says,

"My sheep shall hear my voice and know it." (John 10:27)

One day, in my mind's eye, a voice spoke to me, "Go out onto the twelve acres next to you and claim it, so that it may become what your vision is."

In my vision, I had drawn a Children's Home, a church, a gym, a prayer garden, and a barn. I had drawn my vision on a large piece of cardboard. We were very young Christians at the time, but with tremendous visions. As the Bible says,

"Our young have visions, our old dream dreams." (Act 2:17)

Through the process of time, you can see how I progressed into that category!

Close to midnight, on the seventh night, I woke up to hear that voice inside me saying, "You have one-half hour to claim that land."

I am a very factual person and I was afraid *not* to do what the voice said. These were the instructions, "Braid your hair, (at that time my hair was down to my waist), go down to the barn, and get the pony that we found. Go over to the land and claim it." I followed each direction with care, keeping my main goal in mind.

The cornfields had just been plowed and the ground disked to fertilize for next year's crop. As I walked across the land, I noticed the dirt was so fine that it went in between my toes, feeling smooth and warm. I walked directly toward the middle of the land; then without warning, I saw a cross. I thought to myself, "Now that is ridiculous, I surely don't see any cross out here!"

As I turned around, I realized that the light post in my yard and the weather vane on the garage formed a cross in the moonlight. I knew they would do that whether there was a building there or not. Then, I saw this bright light. I thought, "I am getting out of here!"

As quickly as I could, I ran back. I took the pony to the barn, ran back to the house, and jumped quickly into bed. No one knew what had happened and I didn't tell anyone.

Some years later, my daughter hired a plumber to come to her house. He asked her, "Your mother is at the One Way Farm, isn't she?" She confirmed who I was, whereby he replied, "I don't tell people about this, but when I was about fourteen years old, I was going by the farm and saw this bright light over that land. I never told anyone about it until I ran into another guy and we started talking about One Way Farm. He said he had been fishing at the lake, right by the gravel pit that runs along the road by the house. He saw this bright light and he never went back to fish again."

That story was a confirmation to me that God constantly comes and puts little reminders in front of you: Who is in control? Who is going to assist you? Who is going to hold your hand? Who is going to wipe away the tears? Who, among all else, loves you unconditionally? Jesus Christ does.

Not too long after that I saw surveyors on the land. I could not believe there were surveyors on the land! They told me the land was now for sale. Regrettably, at that time I had no contributors, so I said, "The land can't go up for sale, because I don't have any money right now." Much to my delight, he told me that the owners were willing to negotiate the land contract.

With no time to spare, I found a contributor who was willing to place thirty thousand dollars into an escrow account to hold the land, and that became my first financial obligation...and experience. The contract was signed and full payment of seventy-seven thousand dollars was expected within three years. I really didn't think about what all this meant, I just knew God had put someone in line to save this land for us.

Soon after, we began the process of raising money, so we could build a children's shelter on the land that was just acquired. I had ten children in my house and we desperately needed more space. Plus, I had twenty more children at another facility. Not only did we have children with needs, but I was working day and night without a break. I spent much of my time at speaking engagements or anything else I could do to introduce One Way Farm.

At one of my presentations, a nice gentleman approached me, introducing himself as a building inspector. He said, "I know a man who I think can help you. I think he can get people to help build the shelter." Building the shelter was of the utmost importance because laws had changed and we didn't know what to expect or do. There were stipulations, building codes, along with a few other items that we could not meet.

After making the appropriate arrangements, we met for lunch. Just as we were getting toward the middle of lunch, and as we were explaining to the gentleman what we needed, he said, "I am too busy to do this." Then, he got up and left. That was that.

If you think that incident was unpleasant, it wasn't near as bad as the one I suffered the night before. I went to a zoning meeting about building the shelter, when screaming and yelling began from people protesting the building of the shelter. A man even came up to me and spit in my face. What this man didn't know was that I could relate to another person who was spit in the face...my Lord.

It was then that I really started to wonder if this shelter would ever be. When the gentleman walked out on me at the luncheon, I was really confused. I thought "What does the Lord want of me? I do not understand this." In addition to all of this, I had to find three thousand dollars to meet payroll, which I did not have. The man spitting in my face, the man walking out on me at lunch, payroll problems; I was totally relying on faith to take care of the whole situation.

During all of the commotion and disrespect that I had endured lately, a couple, who I had known for years, came into the office to visit with me. They had lost their children and now they were living on the streets. Both of them were not well; in their health, family, or otherwise. She found out that she had cancer, on top of everything else that was deteriorating in their lives.

We sat there and talked about the years, how hard they had been, and how they were going to try and get their children back. It was right at that moment, my administrative assistant said, "Barbara, I'm sorry to interrupt, but there is someone here to see you." Of course, I didn't want to be rude to my visitors, so I told her to have them wait until I was finished.

We just kept right on talking, and the couple told me how much they appreciated that no matter what time it was, I always had time to talk to them and encourage them. My assistant called again, but this time she said, "Barbara, he is in a Mercedes." I still replied, "He will just have to wait!"

When my assistant called yet again, this couple said, "We better go. This man must really want to see you. However, before we go, the Lord told us you need three thousand dollars." They laid the three thousand dollars on my desk and said, "We have just inherited an estate." You see, the scripture was really coming true. It says,

"Don't invite the wealthy in, but covet those that are poor and in need." (Luke 14:12)

The couple left through the halls of the office; the filth was evident on them, the poverty was evident on them. Then, the man of wealth, with his Mercedes parked outside, passed by them, as he walked toward me. Well, what do you know! It was the gentleman who had lunch with me the day before!

As he sat down, he said he took my literature home, read it, and wanted to talk to me about the shelter. After his departure at lunch I was certain that he was going to say that he wasn't going to help me with the shelter. Surprisingly, he told me he would help. Praise God. Now, we had someone to help us build the shelter.

He sat right there in my office and wrote a check out for one hundred thousand dollars. You see, you never know what God is thinking. We think earthly and factual, but faith is good.

As we began to build the house, someone stopped by and told me that if I planned on building any other houses, I would have to build them right away, because the city was going to incorporate the property, and I wouldn't be able to build any additional housing once that happened.

I did not know what to do with that information except to tell the gentleman helping us. Just as I watched God work before, he replied, "We were going to call you. My wife decided that she wanted to build one of those houses, too." Thank you, Lord!

I received another check for one-hundred thousand dollars from the generous gentleman. You see, you just can't out-think God. What he has planned, how he perceives things, how he uses zonings, how he uses incorporations, and how all those things went together to create One Way Farm.

Our land is divided between the City of Fairfield and Fairfield Township. The shelters and barn are in the Township, while the driveway and Chapel are in the City of Fairfield. Although that separation can be confusing at times, it amazes me that the Lord knew that we needed it that way. Our shelters were located in Fairfield Township, so that we could have wells dug to provide water. Ironically, if the children fall in the house, we call the Township for medical assistance. If they fall in the driveway, we call the City.

God bless thy sleep at night in peace.

Chapter 32
Easter Went to Shawnee Forest

This short story is about spring break, twenty boys, and two men who offered to go with me. One of the men was a Vietnam Veteran who had lost one leg; the other one looked a lot like Rosie Greer who was a big man.

As we started out our trip, we had an agreement that I would walk with all of the children, while they would take the shorter, fire trails and set up camp.

The children did not like the fact that they would have to walk along the longer trails. They didn't understand why they couldn't use the fire trails, but it was quite obvious why they couldn't. The trails of Shawnee Forest are sadistic; the trails are up and down, and can be unpredictable. I remember walking those trails years before and I grabbed hold of a dead tree. When it pulled loose, I fell until I hit the next tree.

During our time away, I gave my staff vacation time for spring break, while I would take all of the children. Spring break usually came at Easter time. This year, it was Easter when we arrived at our camp site. When we got settled in, one of the boys asked me, "What are we going to do, it's Easter?" I replied, "What do you think we ought to do?" He suggested we make crosses, which, of course, I thought was a perfect idea.

Some of the boys began to pick up little sticks, and looking for items to put them together; all working very quietly. All of a sudden, out of the woods came one of the boys, dragging a huge cross that he had made. It was held together with the belt from his pants. I asked, "What are you going to do with that?" He said, "I am going to put it on top of the highest tree on this hill, so that anyone who comes here at Easter time will be able to see that cross."

The other boys began to join in; one by one hoisting him up. They gave him their belts and he began to climb the tree. As he reached the top of the tree, you could see the other boys helping to hold the cross up. They were able to belt the cross to the very top of a tree. When they came back down, their mood was one of silence and reverence.

Two to three years later, I got a call. It was the boy who put the cross in the top of the tree. He told me that he was getting married and on his honeymoon. He wanted to go back to that forest and show his bride the cross in the tree. That moment, which seemed so simple, was a permanent memory for him. I imagine that, by now, he has probably taken his children to see that cross in the tree.

How many other campers on Easter, or any time when the trees have shed their leaves, can see that cross? They must wonder who put that cross in that tree. Simply…it was just a boy.

Chapter 33
My Heart's Desire

People are so busy trying to keep every part of their day running smoothly; trying to take care of children, striving to be a good person, employee, mate, while attempting to meet everyone's needs of the day. You may have your own children in school, but the Bible says,

> "…be about the Lord's work first, and I will give you your heart's desire." (Psalm 37:4)

I have a son who is developmentally disabled and I also have a son who is a genius. One day my son, Adam, who is developmentally disabled, came home with an invitation. The card was an invitation to a luncheon and it came with a white carnation. I asked, "What is this?" He did not know, so I called the school and asked them about it.

Good news! My son, Adam, had fulfilled all of the requirements necessary for a student to be entered into The National Honor Society. The recommendations that came from his teachers and principals at school were exceptional.

On Adam's big day, I attended the luncheon, along with all of his brothers and sisters. We watched him proudly light the candle and receive the purple carnation that gave tribute to his achievement. For his siblings to sit there and watch their brother receive such an honor was magnificent. This moment was a tremendous heart's desire for me. I wanted so badly for Adam to excel and exceed, and so, *be about the Lord's work first, and He will give you your heart's desire.*

Although this poem doesn't coincide with the story I just told you, I thought perhaps you would appreciate it. I remember the table in the hall, and most of all the children who used it.

The Table in the Hall

"I'm the table in the hall
Where I like it most of all.
Some people probably don't know I'm here in the hall.
I hold the special foods for all occasions.
For some, I am the one who catches their books.
As you can see, I show it by my looks.
My wooden edges are worn in a certain spot,
For that is where they use the phone a lot.
Oh, I've had them jump and sit on me,
But I'm strong, for I come from a great pine tree.
I hear their laughter and voices aglow,
I hear the things no others know.
I get waxed every other day.
That is so my mistress can say,
'This is my favorite table you know.'
Then I will shine and my grace will show.
I'm the table in the hall,
I'm in the greatest place of all.
Where I can see the children large and small.
I'm the table in the hall,
Where I like it most of all."

~ Barbara J. Condo

Chapter 34
Over Jordan

In the early 1980's, many of our friends were going to the Holy Land for a visit. We were young in the ministry of God and had no funds with which to travel. Our friends would bring back items made of olive trees, while we could only hope that someday we could travel there, too.

A gentleman who had been working with our ministry said to me, "I think the Lord would like you to be baptized in the Jordan." In the same moment, he offered to pay for us to take a trip to Israel. I could hardly believe it! We would be walking where Christ walked! The trip was great, and after a 17-hour flight, we arrived in Tel Aviv, Israel.

This man blessed us not only with the trip, but he had provided the group with a tour guide to take us everywhere; from a camel ride to visiting the Church of the Nativity. The guide cautioned our group not to get separated from the tour because certain sections were still under Palestinian control. As we stood in line with the many other visitors waiting to enter this magnificent church, a tall, thin man, garbed in tattered native dress, suddenly grabbed my arm.

"Holy One, Holy One," he kept saying, as I followed his lead. I was dazed and falling down to the catacombs of the Church as he continued to take me wherever he wanted to go. When we reached our destination, I stood in front of fifteen-foot wooden doors. As the doors opened, much to my surprise, there stood a Greek Orthodox priest at an altar! The man, who had pulled me down the catacombs to the doors, began exclaiming again, "Holy One, Holy One."

The priest was dressed in black, his head was covered, and there was a huge cross hanging around his neck. He was holding a bottle of oil in one hand and a candle in the other. As he walked toward me, I began to get frightened. What was happening?

The priest reached his hand out toward me, gave me the oil, and said, "Take this and go heal your people." He handed me the candle and said to me, "Let this be a light unto your path."

As soon as the priest stopped speaking, the man who had led me to the catacombs grabbed my arm, dragging me up the many marble steps and back into the line waiting to enter the Church. Dazed and confused, I began to explain what had just happened to my group.

The tour guide said, "No one is allowed there. Only the Holiest of Holy are allowed." I stood with oil and candle in total amazement as to what had just happened. I kept the oil and candle close to me, and used them until there was nothing left.

When the oil seemed to be used up, I poured what was left into my hands, asking God to imbed the oil into my pores and release it whenever I needed a miracle. I have anointed my checkbook for a donation, I have anointed people, places, things, and my faith has been taken to the people; with the oil to confirm the blessing.

My work is a light unto their path. And, yes, I was baptized in the Jordan.

Chapter 35
Tragedy #1

In life, there are several times you may ask yourself, "Why, Lord?" I had been married for twenty-eight years, but this great miracle had come to a standstill. My husband had retired, and I thought he would look forward to spending many days of golf with my son, Adam, who, as you know, is developmentally disabled. Regrettably, Adam also thought that was the plan.

One day, and without notice, my husband announced that he was leaving. He said that his life plans had changed and he had to go. I was shocked and devastated. Adam and I did not fit into his life anymore. He left, and Adam and I were so upset with the turn of events. We had very little with just the two of us and I wasn't quite sure how we were going to care for each other.

As life started to get back to some sort of order, I thought I should allow Adam to have his own apartment; in hopes that the change would give him the feeling that he was an adult. Plus, I didn't know if the house was going to go, too, due to the fact that I now found myself single.

As time went on, things started to get even worse. The only way I was going to survive this setback was to auction off everything that I had. I knew the One Way Farm needed money, too.

For over thirty years I had collected items that I thought might be worth something someday. Some of the items were very old, like the Richard Nixon's cufflinks, which I found in a flea market for fifty cents, and root beer bottles that had floated down the Ohio River in 1927, which surprisingly still had the root beer in them. The value of my collectables and antiques, insurance wise, was probably well over one hundred sixty-four thousand dollars, but sadly, I only got nine thousand.

I felt as if I could not go on. I knew I had to figure out what was happening or what I was doing wrong. The green and pink glassware in the collection was Depression ware that came from my grandmother. I only had a three-quarter bed, a TV, and a recliner left. The worse had come to pass. I must sell the house.

My biggest fear was now in front me. Where would I live? I remember saying to my spirit, "I don't really need anything, just my clothes...just my clothes, please." I thought perhaps I could sleep in the basement of the multipurpose building. I could put a small bed down there.

As I pondered over where I was going to live, a dear friend of mine who had purchased some of our things said to me, "The Lord does not want you sleeping in the basement of a building." He told me how he could get the building & loan to release one of the two acres of land I had, which gave me the funds I needed to build. He told me that he would build the house and bill me only for the cost of the materials. There it stood; a three-bedroom house with a basement. God had delivered me from nothing to something very wonderful. There sat a wonderful house, and at a price I could afford.

I did not have any furniture, but I remembered a gentleman who had become a Christian, I had baptized him in a pool, and he had a furniture store. So off to the store I went to talk to him. I only had about fifteen hundred dollars left on the credit card after I let the Farm use my cards for food and gas. I needed whatever that amount would buy.

The Lord had given me a house, and now it was time for the furniture. I was only expecting a good price, never was I expecting the following miracles. These next miracles came in small and large packages and they were all blessings from our heavenly Father.

I went to the furniture store, and started out the conversation with the man learning the rest of my story; how the Lord had blessed me with the house, how I had to auction off everything, and that I just needed furniture for the new home. Normally, I wouldn't share my hard luck story, but at the time I did so because not only was I in crisis, but the Farm was in crisis, too. Money was in high demand, both personally and professionally. I gave One Way Farm permission to use my personal charge cards to pay the expenses they had and to purchase food. I knew the Lord would not forsake me.

As we started to talk about the furniture, I saw a bedroom set that I really loved. I knew I could probably only afford the chest of drawers, but when I asked about it, he replied, "I don't break up a set." I then asked, "How much is the set?" "Nineteen ninety-five" he replied. Well, that wasn't going to work so we headed over to look at tables and chairs for the kitchen.

The salesman said, "Oh, I have a kitchen set here, and because of the glass, nobody will buy it. You can have it." Praise God, there is the table!

Before I could contain myself, he continued, "By the way, I have another table you could use in the basement and I have a hutch I will give you. Let's go look at the living room furniture."

All my life, I wanted white furniture, but with having so many children, I never had anything white. It just happened to be that he had a beautiful love seat and chair…and they were white. To my delight, they were fifteen hundred dollars.

As we continued to check out the white furniture, I decided that I did not need any living room furniture. The money could go to a better use. All of sudden, he said, "Look at it! It has a black mark on each piece, I can't sell those! You can have those too!" It was as if an angel had taken a magic marker and put a dot on the couch and the chair. There was my table and hutch for my kitchen, my table for the basement, and my living room furniture. The Lord had provided me with all that I needed. I remember just sitting and crying. Here I was; I went from nowhere to go to a home with furniture and faith in God.

You can have what your heart desires, if you believe. The Lord was the only thing I had to believe in.

When the truck came to my house, as they began to unload the furniture, here came the bedroom set; not just the dresser, but all of the pieces! That was the gift that filled my house. My house of Glory.

Chapter 36
Tragedy #2

Time is passing and I am trying as hard as I can to create a faith-based home for the children in need. With all of the hardships that came our way, it was not always the easiest task to complete. But, with time and effort I believe we continue to do good work for the Lord.

One day, while I was sitting in my office with one of our counselors sitting across from me, something odd began to happen. Unknowingly, my eyes had changed color and began to swell. "You look ill," she said. Almost instantly, I became very confused. The counselor gently took me to the car and drove me to Mercy South Hospital; checking my pulse as she drove.

I remember telling her that I didn't want to go. Her statement to me was, "My husband, when he had a heart attack, looked just like you are looking." She must have been right because I woke up at Deaconess Hospital after open-heart surgery.

After a long bout of healing, I came home to loads of care and prayers. My friends sat up around the clock watching over me. Every four hours someone new would come to stay with me. Still, during my healing process, I was instilled in the ministry that we were work-ing for. I began to share with those watching over me how the Lord had blessed me and about the walk I had walked for years. Each one seemed to have a special need, mostly in need of prayer for their particular needs and a hug goodbye; then, they were on their way.

Soon, I was back on my feet, working everyday. I was back to giving children and case workers my time, speaking for donations at lunch and in the evenings, and continually trying to raise the millions of dollars needed to continue One Way Farm's mission. The journey seemed nearly impossible at times, but I would just say, and still do,

"The Lord has, and will provide, whether it is money or macaroni and cheese." Soon, I was back on my feet and feeling the pressures of the financial burden releasing. There were buildings to build, like our Thrift Store for one.

Just as life was looking up for One Way, a dear friend of mine called with very bad news. He had a CAT scan done, which showed nodules were found on one of his lungs. I dreamt that the surgery was performed, but that his skin was pulled away from his body and then put back in place. This visual disturbed me, so I went to my friend's house and asked if I could pray for him.

As I put my hands on his feet, I could feel the power of God through his body. We said our goodbyes and I left. Monday came and his surgery was scheduled right away. Everyone was so nervous; he had been a heavy cigar smoker. What was going to happen to him?

After many hours of waiting, a call came. The doctors had gone in to do the surgery, but there wasn't anything there. There were no nodules to be found so they just sewed him back up. This event was never mentioned, but the wonders that the Lord allows is our blessing.

Two months later, after my friend had time to heal, I went to lunch with him. I explained that I needed to build a barn so we could have a Thrift Store. Later that day he called and asked, "How much is the barn?" "It is twenty-five thousand dollars," I replied. "I will buy it," he answered. That is the way miracles work.

"Ask, and you shall receive." (Matthew 7:7) "Go about the Lord's work first..." (Psalm 37:4-5), "He shall give you your heart's desire. Faith is evidence of things hoped for, and evidence of things not yet seen." (Hebrews 11:1)

One Way Farm is such a miracle in everyday life, and for the people who work here, their lives are changed, too.

Chapter 37
Tragedy #3

We needed funds desperately, but due to an incident that happened in our county, hardly anyone was donating. I remember during Christmas of 2006, we lost sixty thousand dollars due to the incident, and we were in no way involved in it. The total loss we incurred was one-hundred fifty-nine thousand dollars; we needed to have a yard sale.

First, there was one tent, and then there were two. As people heard we were trying to raise money to keep the One Way Farm Children's Home open, they began to bring truckloads of items. Then, there were four tents, finally five tents, and two large walk-in containers. We raised ten thousand dollars, not near what we needed, but a gift all the same.

In the midst of all this commotion, I started feeling very dizzy. The temperature was in the nineties and the feeling that I was going to faint got even stronger. I went home, but began to feel a deep pressure in my chest. Unknowingly, I was in cardiac arrest. One of the major arteries in my heart had collapsed. I woke up hazy and in my confusion they were asking me to sign for blood.

I felt my stomach swelling, as I began to vomit blood. Not long after that I was told that I had a cut artery, and my stomach was swelling, filling with blood. I needed more blood.

In the middle of everything, the bright light approached again, as it had done several times before in my life. The same men were talking; one claimed he was taking my life, the other stating, "No one can do that. Only I can take her life."

This time my health was dragging me down; making it difficult to determine whether I would live. After nine days in Intensive Care, I demanded to be released to go home. All they said was "You are a single, seventy-year-old woman. Who will take care of you?" I replied, "I'm going home and that is that." I didn't want to stay; especially when they started to talk to me about a nursing home. The nurses told my doctor to be prepared…that I was going home. Yes, I went home.

I know now that I was in no condition to go home, although the Lord had given me a hand maiden two years prior to this event. She was a young, developmentally disabled African-American girl who I had found sick and in need of my care. That was when I took her into my home. With my return home from the hospital, she decided to make a bed on the floor next to me so she could hold my hand. That way she would know when I needed water or when I needed to go to the bathroom.

For six months she slept on the floor, slowly leading me to my recliner so I could accomplish some work during the day. I would have my supervisors come over and we would try to keep business going as usual. All of my speaking engagements were rescheduled with the explanation of my illness, or board members and friends spoke in my place. Slowly, I began to heal.

As time continued on, I would get up and, with help, get dressed and go to work. My coworkers would carry me in and place me on my couch. I even had to have the phones moved because the couch was so far from my desk.

Days and months went by: January, February, March, and April. I seemed to be okay, except for walking. In May, I went to walk out of my front door and my legs would not work. This was all due to the six strokes I had during surgery. With no ability to walk, I fell off my porch, two steps down, face first, and slid onto the cement. I knew I was hurt.

In my confusion, I could hear Andrea trying to help me. I could feel the blood and heard the staff members calling the Life Squad. "We called the Life Squad." I heard people say, although I was really dazed.

When I arrived at the hospital, the staff checked the bleeding immediately. The nurse in attendance said, "I'm going to put some Novocain into your entire face. You have a tremendous amount of damage." My eyes, mouth, and face were swollen and bruised. After a short hospital stay, I was able to go back home and try it again.

After more healing, I once again began to work on my mission of the grace of God. I went to work, day after day, and I was getting stronger. I anointed myself with oil and I lay hands on myself. "Lord, I must get better." I prayed. One Thursday night I heard a voice,

"My sheep shall hear my voice and know it." (John 10:27)

It was not mud in the blind man's eyes that healed him; it was an act of faith. "Have your family take you to the river. Put a rope around you, you shall walk out."

The Big Miami River runs about four-hundred feet from my house and at that time the Miami was in full flood stage. The water was moving fast. I could not walk, but my family carried me to the river; placing me in the river up to my knees. I was amazed, the water felt so warm. A little time went by, the man who helped take me to the river, said, "I can't leave you out here in the river." I assured him that I would be alright. Almost instantly, he shouted, "Here comes a tree!" Out of my peripheral vision, I could see a tree heading my way. Not a branch, but an entire tree coming down the river, heading directly toward me. I knew I had better get out of the river or be gone. So, I ran out of the river.

The helpful man was still standing there in the water, disbelieving what he was seeing. I yelled to him, "Get out of the river, there is a tree coming!" He got out of the river, still stunned in amazement; I could walk!

We went back to the house on our own two feet. No cane or walker was needed. It took about twenty-four hours for me to realize that I had been healed. I did not have to hold onto the walls, I could walk. I could walk!

On the following Monday, I walked into my office. My staff could hardly believe their eyes. When I explained that the Lord had healed me and I am forever in His care. The poem "The Footprints" is true in my life. I just sit and wonder how I ever got where I am today.

His love is more than you or I can repay. His understanding is far beyond belief. Won't you seek Him today? If you would read such a testimony as this, would you not go just one step further, and say, "Yes, Jesus, I'm coming home."

CONCLUSION

Barbara has come a long way in life and in her love to God. Her health is doing just fine, and as of June 16, 2011 she is still a vibrant, intelligent, 74-year-old woman. Each day, she wakes at 5:30 in the morning and has breakfast at the Waffle House, located in Fairfield. You can see her joined by her companion, Elvis, her loving dog, as she makes her way through her daily routine. She works hard to do whatever is needed for One Way Farm Children's Home. Whether it is talking to the children or speaking to raise the funds for the children. Please come and stay for a visit. Stop by and see a vision and a dream.

AUTOBIOGRAPHY

Barbara grew up in Appalachian Kentucky before moving to Ohio. She has five children of her own, but has always found room for more than just her own.

In 1976, with a powerful desire to help others, and only fifty-nine dollars in her pocket, she created One Way Farm Children's Home, located in Fairfield, Ohio. All she knew for certain was that she had a mission; to provide a home to the homeless. Initially, she provided a home for adult parolees, but in this loving atmosphere her farmhouse was soon overflowing.

At the suggestion of a Juvenile Detention Center chaplain, Barbara gradually shifted her focus to the prevention of broken lives; and so she began working exclusively with children of all ages. Her first children's home began in Fairfield, which soon expanded to include a home for boys in Somerville, Ohio in 1980. Eventually, both homes were combined on the Fairfield campus.

One Way Farm Children's Home houses boys and girls; each building carrying the unique sentiment of their guests. Approximately eighty-five hundred children have lived at One Way Farm Children's Home in the past thirty-three years.

One Way Farm Children's Home mends the minds, bodies, and spirits of children.

Barbara is an accomplished survivor with great leadership talents; proving that although life can bring you down, you never give up on your dreams. Many have recognized her endeavors by presenting her with the following awards and recognitions:

2010
Steel Magnolia Award honoring women who have faced personal adversity and have shown exceptional leadership through their work in the community

2010
Formally Recognized by the State of Ohio House of Representatives
For years of work and service to the community

2009
ATHENA Award as presented by Cincy Magazine in recognition of professional women who have achieved professional excellence, given back to their community & created leadership opportunities for other women

2009
Formally Recognized by the State of Ohio Senate
For years of work and service to the community

2009
Inducted into the Senior Citizens Hall of Fame
State of Ohio

2009
Janet Clemmons/SELF Community Service Award Nominee
Butler County, Ohio

2009
Jefferson Award Nominee

2008
"Be the Scream" Provider Award

2007
1st Masonic District of Ohio
Community Service Award

2006
City of Fairfield, Hall of Fame

2005
Business Person of the Year Award
Fairfield Chamber of Commerce
2004
Women of Excellence Award
Southeastern Butler County Chamber of Commerce

2002
Secret of Living in Giving Award
Smith Family Foundation

2001
Leading Women in Community Service Honoree
Leading Women, Inc.

2001
2000 Partner Award
Guardian Savings Bank

2000
Key to the City
City of Fairfield

2000
Millennium Honor Roll
(10 total selected to represent 45 years of city history)
City of Fairfield

2000
Outstanding Women of Achievement in Butler County
YMCA

1992
President's Volunteer Action Award Nominee
President Ronald Reagan

1984
Woman of the Year
Cincinnati Enquirer
1982
Sertoma Service to Mankind Award
Southwest Ohio District

1980-1981
Business Administration
Southern Ohio College

1980
Beta Sigma Phi International First Lady of the Year
Beta Sigma Phi

1980
Fairfield Woman of the Year
City of Fairfield

1976 to present
Founder/Executive Director
One Way Farm Children's Home